HOW TO WRITE E

In this Series

Other titles in preparation

WRITE
BUSINESS LETTERS

A practical introduction for everyone

Ann Dobson

How To Books

Other books by the same author

How to Communicate at Work
How to Manage an Office
How to Return to Work

British Library Cataloguing in Publication Data
A catalogue record for this book is available from the British Library.

© Copyright 1995 by Ann Dobson.

First published in 1995 by How To Books Ltd, Plymbridge House, Estover Road, Plymouth PL6 7PZ, United Kingdom. Tel: (01752) 735251/695745. Fax: (01752) 695699. Telex: 45635.

Note: The material contained in this book is set out in good faith for general guidance and no liability can be accepted for loss or expense incurred as a result of relying in particular circumstances on statements made in the book. The laws and regulations are complex and liable to change, and readers should check the current position with the relevant authorities before making personal arrangements.

Typeset by PDQ Typesetting, Stoke-on-Trent
Printed and bound by The Cromwell Press, Broughton Gifford, Melksham, Wiltshire SN12 8PH.

Contents

PART 2: SAMPLE LETTERS

Contents

List of illustrations

Preface

There is a big need for a simple, easy to follow guide to writing business letters, if only to dispel the myth that business letters are complicated and very time consuming to write. The layout of a business letter has become considerably simplified in recent years. The content of the letter need not be complicated or lengthy. On the contrary: the modern approach is to be brief and to the point, using simple language that everyone can understand. *How to Write Business Letters* offers this modern, simplified approach to create clear, effective letters. These are the letters that get results today.

In Part 1 of the book the basic principles of business letters are discussed: why letters are necessary, their planning and presentation, the use of technology and guidelines to essential grammar and punctuation are all included, to help the reader plan his or her own letters. Realistic examples are given throughout. Part 2 shows sample letters to cover most business needs. Case studies are used in Part 2 to show how letters can be effective or non-effective according to how they are written.

This book has been prepared in an easy to understand way designed for use by anyone. Whether you are a school leaver, a student, an employed or self-employed worker, a 'returner' to work, or a person at home, *How to Write Business Letters* aims to provide you with both an interesting book to read and a valuable reference guide.

Throughout Chapters 6–11, three fictional companies and characters are used to illustrate the difference between a good letter and a bad letter, in terms of clarity, effectiveness and accuracy of content.

Using these three imaginary organisations and personnel, every sample letter is displayed twice, with comments after each example. Hopefully these comments will show just how important it is to write effective business letters.

Ann Dobson

Is This You?

Job seeker   Householder

        School leaver

Accounts assistant   College leaver

        Sales clerk

Advertiser   Sales manager

        Order clerk

Typist   Publicity assistant

        Despatch clerk

Invoice clerk   Purchase ledger clerk

        Receptionist

Office junior   University graduate

        Retired person

The boss   Management trainee

        Personnel officer

Office temp   Word processing clerk

        Secretary

Personal assistant   Export/import assistant

        Returner to work

Student   Club secretary

        Shop owner

Business partner   Departmental manager

        PTA secretary

Supervisor   Customer services assistant

        Entrepreneur

Self employed   Secretarial assistant

        Builder

Clerical assistant   Painter and decorator

        Factory owner

Insurance agent   Irate member of public

        Business executive

Fig. 1. Is this you? – some of today's business letter writers.

1
The Business Letter

WHY WRITE A LETTER AT ALL?

In this modern age of electronic marvels, the rather dated sounding 'business letter' may seem out of place. After all, a business letter takes time and effort to prepare, and another method of communication, such as a telephone call or a scribbled message, may sometimes be just as effective.

In very many other instances, however, the business letter is just as important today as it was twenty, thirty or even forty years ago. It seeks to organise, inform and make things happen and it is an extremely valuable means of communication. In addition, if properly prepared, a letter will give a favourable impression of the company or organisation it represents. This favourable impression could lead to a long and successful business association.

The benefits of a business letter

- A permanent record which can be referred to later.

- The opportunity to plan, organise and draft the contents.

- The chance to deal with complex and lengthy subjects.

- Evidence, should it be needed, in a Court of Law.

- A means of transmitting confidential information.

WHAT ABOUT THE ALTERNATIVES?

As we have already mentioned, there will be times when a formal business letter is not really necessary. Let us take a look at the alternatives and when they should be used.

Writing a memorandum (or memo)

A memorandum or memo is used very widely in the business world today. In fact cynics might say that memo-writing keeps some organisations in business!

Like a business letter, a memo is a formal method of communication. The main function of a memo is to pass information from one department to another or one person to another, within the same organisation.

Most large organisations have their own printed memo forms to use. They may look similar to the following example:

MEMORANDUM

To

From

Ref

Date

When the memo has been completed it looks like this:

MEMORANDUM

To   All Staff

From   James Smith – Managing Director

Ref   JS/MY

Date   21 October 19–.

HOLIDAY ARRANGEMENTS – CHRISTMAS 19–

This is to inform you all that we shall be closing from Friday 20 December until Wednesday 2 January. You will not be required to take any of these days as part of your holiday entitlement.

We hope that as a result of this long Christmas break staff will not ask for holiday leave during December and January except in very exceptional circumstances.

Writing a message

Instead of using a formal letter or memo, a good deal of information can be passed by means of simple handwritten or typed messages. Messages do not look as pleasing to the eye as well displayed business letters or memos, but they are a useful means of sending simple information from one place to another without any frills.

Using a printed business document

When an order is placed for goods, or payment is being made for goods received, it is not always necessary to send a letter. Many organisations will have printed documents such as

- headed order forms

- estimates and quotations

- invoices

- statements

- requisitions

and so on, which can be used for routine business communications.

Making a telephone call

How would we ever manage in the business world of today without the telephone? We have all come to rely on it for so much of our daily communication both at home and at work.

The use of the telephone removes the need for much of our written communication. A telephone conversation gives us an instant reaction from the other person. Decisions can be made in seconds or minutes. Actions can be explained, apologies can be made, arguments can be fought.

What the telephone does not provide us with, however, is a written record. For example, it is little use moaning about non-delivery of some goods and saying to the company, 'Well, your Mr Smith agreed to let us have the goods on Friday,' unless you have proof of that agreement in writing.

The telephone can be used:

- For transmitting simple information to another person or organisation.

- For informal discussions.

- For speed, where a letter would not be fast enough.

- For all information that does not need to be permanently recorded.

The face to face spoken word

If you speak to someone face to face, you will be able to see their reaction, judge their mood, and usually get a good indication of what is to happen next. It is, however, often not a practical proposition if long distances are involved.

Meetings can be just a chance encounter in the corridor – more of a 'chat' really – or a formal meeting involving several people. A meeting of any sort is usually a successful way of exchanging ideas and information quickly. Decisions can be reached there and then; in a formal meeting, notes or minutes can be taken to provide a written record.

The chance encounter in the corridor can provide instant answers, unlike a memo or other forms of internal notes.

Example

John, a Sales Manager in a dog food company, has received a complaint from a retail outlet about one of his reps. As he is on his way to lunch, he sees Molly, the rep in question. The following conversation takes place:

'Molly, I've been looking for you. Can I have a quick word? Where are you off to?' John falls in step with Molly as she is walking along the corridor towards the stairs.

'Hi, John. I'm just off to lunch, actually. Let's have a word outside shall we? There's a bench just round here.' Molly leads the way outside and round to a vacant bench in the company grounds. They sit down.

'Right Molly. I've had a 'phone call from Sunny Stores this morning. I don't mind telling you, I was a little upset at what Mrs Spall told me.' John looks at Molly expectantly, waiting for her answer. Much to his surprise Molly starts to laugh.

'Let me guess. She said I hadn't processed her last order for Doggybest. Shall I tell you why?'

John nods and Molly carries on.

'We have had trouble over the last six months with them paying for their orders. I didn't tell you because I thought Dave and I had it under control. Each time there has been trouble he has gone in and they have paid up. Until now that is. This time they won't pay and we have said they can't have any more goods until they do. It is company policy after all, isn't it?'

'Well yes, it is. She didn't mention any non-payment to me, of course. But it would have helped if I had known the situation. You and Dave should not keep this sort of thing to yourselves you know.' John is, at the same time, pleased that there is an answer to the problem, but cross that he has not been kept informed.

'I know. I'm sorry, John. I was going to tell you, but you are always so busy. I did try once but you said to come back another time.' Molly defends her actions in the best way she can.

'Okay, well I'm sorry I said that to you. As you know, I am always busy, but I shall make sure everyone knows that I will make time for them whenever it is necessary, so that embarrassing situations like this do not occur again.' John gets up, smiles at Molly and sends her off for her lunch.

This conversation has been very useful. Firstly it has explained the situation with regard to Sunny Stores. Secondly, it has highlighted to John that his staff have found him unapproachable of late. It is now up to him to improve relationships with his team. These improved relationships will probably include the need for more internal written communication, if he does not always find the time for a 'chat'. Finally it has highlighted the need for a business letter to be sent to Sunny Stores now to sort out the problem.

USING MODERN TECHNOLOGY

Technology can be used in a number of ways to make letter writing easier and less time-consuming.

Firstly, we can store standard paragraphs on a computer, so that letters can be produced quickly without the need for any writing or dictating first. Whilst standard paragraphs are fine for basic letters they are not suitable for individual complex matters which do not fit into any 'standard' category. There is also the danger that the wrong standard paragraphs can be selected by the operator, often with disastrous results!

Pre-printed standard letters and forms are very useful for routine, mass produced, business correspondence, but they cannot be easily adapted to other purposes.

Standard paragraphs and letters are looked at in more detail in Chapter 5.

Using the fax machine

As an alternative to the post, many letters and other documents can be transmitted by electronic means. The most commonly used is the facsimile machine, more usually called 'the fax'. The fax machine is similar to a photocopier, in that it makes an exact copy of your document: but unlike a photocopier it can send that document through the telephone network to another fax machine anywhere in the world. Apart from letters, you can also use it to send diagrams, photographs

Working out the cost of a business letter

Cost of time	Hourly cost	Minutes taken	Cost
Drafting the letter	say £10	15 minutes	£2.50
Dictating the letter	say £10	5 minutes	£0.83
Typing the letter and envelope	say £5	5 minutes	£0.42
Checking and signing the letter	say £10	3 minutes	£0.50
Posting the letter and filing copy(ies)	say £5	2 minutes	£0.17

Cost of materials

Headed notepaper	£0.05
Envelope	£0.05
Carbon or photocopies	£0.03
Postage stamp	£0.25
Typewriter ribbon	£0.05

Overheads

Overheads	Hourly cost	Minutes taken	Cost
Office rent and business rates	say £5	30 minutes	£2.50
Heat, light and power			£0.50
Insurance			£0.10
Depreciation of equipment			£0.25

TOTAL COSTS	£8.20

Fig. 2. Working out the cost of a business letter.
What do you think it would cost in your own organisation?

and other technical documents.

How it works
The principle is as follows:

- Two fax machines are linked by means of telephone lines.

- You place the top copy of your letter or document in the tray of your fax machine.

- The recipient's fax number is dialled.

- The recipient's machine reproduces a facsimile of the original.

The big plus point about using a fax is the speed of transmission (almost instantaneous). The minus point is that the quality of the reproduction is not as good as the original, so that non-urgent business letters are still more likely to be sent by post.

WEIGHING UP THE COSTS OF COMMUNICATION

A business letter is expensive to produce and transmit. It is not just a question of taking a piece of A4 headed paper and tapping out a quickly prepared letter.

First of all, unless standard letters or standard paragraphs are being used, the content of the letter has to be written out or dictated to someone else. That can mean the writer's time and the typist/word processing operator's time in producing the letter. Then there is the paper, ribbon or cartridge, and wear and tear on the machinery used. Time needs to be allowed for filing and an allowance made for overhead costs such as heating, lighting and rent.

The decision then has to be made whether the letter is to be faxed or sent by post. In the case of the latter option, an envelope or label will need to be provided together with a stamp.

So you will see that individual personalised letters can cost several pounds to produce, and this must be weighed against, for instance, short telephone calls which may often cost just a few pence. Many businesses today get printouts from the telephone company showing the time and cost of each telephone call, and the number dialled.

All methods of communication have their own special purpose, however, and the cost of each method is just one of the major factors to be considered when deciding how to communicate on a particular occasion.

DATE	END TIME	EXTN	DIALLED NUMBER	CONTRACT	DURATION m:s	COST
20:12:94	11:52	235	9690609		0:36	0.05
20:12:94	12:21	235	903924371S2		25:38	2.40
20:12:94	12:32	235	9690609		10:08	0.40
20:12:94	15:01	235	9690609		0:45	0.05
20:12:94	15:47	235	9690609		17:52	0.70
20:12:94	15:55	235	90386750534		6:30	0.55
20:12:94	17:16	235	90617666500		1:43	0.15
21:12:94	11:18	235	90392460070		14:44	1.35
21:12:94	12:44	235	90225782585		5:55	0.55
21:12:94	13:29	235	9024251S533		42:39	4.00
22:12:94	13:21	235	90714082474		0:43	0.05
22:12:94	14:18	235	90782412694		1:30	0.15
3:01:95	11:27	235	9778547		10:22	0.40
3:01:95	14:22	235	9226226		1:33	0.05
3:01:95	16:18	235	908177118844		0:59	0.10
3:01:95	16:45	235	90718395901		0:37	0.05
3:01:95	16:51	235	90714995443		0:38	0.05
3:01:95	17:01	235	90717307122		0:33	0.05
3:01:95	17:05	235	90715898835		0:45	0.05
3:01:95	17:12	235	90714344371		0:33	0.05
4:01:95	10:37	235	90717341058		2:41	0.25
4:01:95	10:48	235	9192		1:05	0.25
4:01:95	10:48	235	90714864880		0:39	0.05
4:01:95	10:52	235	90719371921		0:27	0.05
4:01:95	10:53	235	90719371921		0:27	0.05
4:01:95	11:00	235	9192		2:47	0.25
4:01:95	11:01	235	908120198978		0:40	0.05

Fig. 3. Example of an itemised list of business telephone charges from British Telecommunications PLC.

MAKING YOUR CHOICE

Now that we have looked at the various ways we can exchange information, the decision has to be taken on whether or not a letter is really necessary. As we have said, the final choice will depend on many factors and should be made after weighing up the pros and cons.

To sum up, if displayed attractively and free from errors, a formal business letter serves as a good 'ambassador' for the company or organisation it represents.

It is also a permanent and, if necessary, confidential record. The necessary information is stated in black and white and, as long as you keep a copy, you will always have proof of the existence of your letter should you need it. For internal correspondence, of course, the same could be said of a memo.

These arguments should be balanced against the fact that a letter takes a good deal of time and money to prepare. This means that an unnecessary letter is uneconomical to produce, however impressive it looks.

Preparation and planning

Whenever a letter is considered to be necessary, the next step is to plan and present your information in the best way possible. Chapters 2 to 5 will give you guidance on this. You will see how to achieve the desired results by preparing simple 'jargon-free' letters – the type that other people can understand and act upon. Word processing systems are discussed, with particular emphasis on how time can be saved by using the various facilities available to best advantage.

By following through the various stages of preparation, you will soon be able to construct your own business letters both speedily and effectively.

CHECKLIST

A letter offers

- A permanent record.

- The opportunity to plan, organise and draft the contents.

- The chance to deal with complex and lengthy subjects.

- Evidence, should it be needed in a court of law.

- A means of transmitting confidential information.

Points to consider

- The available alternatives.
- Whether a letter is the best of these alternatives.
- The cost of producing the letter.
- The best way of sending the letter, ie post or fax.

POINTS FOR DISCUSSION

1   Would you choose to send a letter or make a telephone call in the following situations? Give your reasons.

    (a) To offer someone a job.

    (b) To advise a member of staff of a pay rise.

    (c) To ask a travel agent for information on flight times.

    (d) To check on available dates and times for a meeting with the various people involved.

    (e) To apply for a job from an advertisement giving the telephone number and the address.

2   'Sending business letters is the most important way of communicating between one organisation and another.' Do you agree with this statement? Give reasons for your opinion.

3   Take a business letter you have recently received. Is the meaning clear? Working with a partner, see if you can improve the wording of the letter.

2
How to Master the Basics

THINKING ABOUT THE GRAMMAR

The mention of the word 'grammar' probably reminds you of school and all those 'rules' you were told to learn. At the time you probably didn't think nouns, verbs and adjectives were important at all. However, once you come to writing your own business letters you will see that in order to construct good sentences, a basic knowledge of grammar is very helpful. Only if words are strung together in the correct way will the meaning of sentences be clear for all to read and understand. Good sentence writing is discussed in more detail on page 28.

Understanding the parts of speech
The words that we use are divided into different categories. These categories are known as **parts of speech** and all the main categories have their part to play in the construction of sentences. The most important categories are listed below.

Nouns
A noun is a name of a person or a thing. All sentences should contain a noun or a pronoun. The **subject** of a sentence is always (or always includes) a noun or pronoun.

> *eg* Today **Susan** went out for a walk in Devon.
> The **house** was nestling on the hill.

Only a proper noun (Susan, Devon) needs to begin with a capital letter. Other nouns (house, walk, hill) do not.

Pronouns
A pronoun is a word used instead of a noun.
> *eg* Mary went to work. Later **she** came home.

Verbs
A verb is a 'being' or 'doing' word. It shows action. It says what the subject of a sentence is. Every sentence should contain a verb.

> *eg* Jane **listens** to Peter.
> Rose **walked** with her mother.

Adverbs
An adverb gives more information about a verb.

> *eg* Jane listens **quietly** to Peter.
> Rose walked **quickly** with her mother.

Adjectives
An adjective is a 'describing' word. It gives more information about a noun.

> *eg* The house was **small**.
> Patrick was **tall** and **thin**.

Prepositions
A preposition shows the relationship of a thing or person to another. It is followed by a noun or a pronoun.

> *eg* The vase in the window was different **from** her own.
> Susan was accompanied **by** Peter.
> She did it **for** her friend.

Conjunctions
A conjunction is a joining word.

> *eg* Bill **and** Ben.
> The sky was bright **but** rain was forecast for later.

PUNCTUATING EFFECTIVELY

Effective punctuation is just as important as the correct use of the parts of speech. Full stops, commas, question marks, brackets and many others all have their part to play in helping us form words into well constructed sentences and paragraphs.

The following guidelines should help with punctuation problems.

Capital letters

Use capital letters:

- to begin sentences;

- for proper nouns, eg Susan, Lands End, North Hospital;

- for titles, eg the Prime Minister, the Inland Revenue;

- for certain abbreviations, eg MP (Member of Parliament), FRCS (Fellow of the Royal College of Surgeons).

Otherwise their use is often a matter of choice, but do remember to be consistent.

A full stop

Use a full stop:

- at the end of a sentence.

A full stop can also be used after initials or abbreviations, although the modern trend is not do so. See page 27 for a section on **open punctuation.**

A comma

A comma is the shortest marked pause in a sentence. It is widely used, sometimes too widely.
Use a comma:

- to separate words or short phrases in a list:
  eg The girl had pink, blue, red and white trousers.

- to separate a word or words at the start of a sentence:
  eg Unfortunately, the other man was more suitable.

- to introduce speech:
  eg As he rose to his feet he said, 'Good morning everyone.'

- to separate something inserted in a sentence without changing the meaning:
  eg It was not, therefore, an easy matter to decide.

- to separate words which add an explanation or meaning to the main theme:
  eg Susan James, the class prefect, gave a recital during lunch.

- to make the sentence generally easier to read and to avoid any confusion.

A semicolon

A semicolon shows a longer pause than a comma but shorter than a full stop. It has great value but is rarely used, mainly because it is not fully understood.

Use a semicolon:

- to show a contrast in statements:
  eg Jane liked pop music; her friend preferred jazz.

- to separate items in a list:
  eg The new villas were luxurious: spacious master bedroom with en suite shower; two further double bedrooms; open plan kitchen and lounge area; fenced garden with patio; private swimming pool; full maid service and full board facilities.

- to show statements closely linked in thought:
  eg He hoped she would start behaving herself; otherwise life would never improve.

- to add emphasis:
  eg She stopped; she looked behind her; she started to scream.

A colon

Use a colon:

- to introduce a list:
  eg The books included: The Lost Prayer by Sue Abbott, The Restaurant World by John Sims and Lost by Paul Ase.

- to introduce direct speech or a quotation.
  eg The Speaker began: 'Lords, Ladies and Gentlemen...'

- to show two parts of the same sentence. The second part usually explains the first part.
  eg He looked happy today: he had just learned he was to become a father again.

Parenthesis or round brackets   (   )

Brackets can be useful to enclose words adding an extra meaning to a sentence. If the brackets are removed, the sentence should still make sense.

  eg John Jones (our new neighbour) will be coming to the meeting next week.

Square brackets [ ]

Use square brackets:

- to show an addition to a direct quotation.

    eg Mr Hands addressed the meeting as follows: 'Hello everyone. I hope that you [the employees] will enjoy the meeting this evening.'

The hyphen -

The most common use of the hyphen used to be to join two words together so that they were looked upon as one. Nowadays the hyphen in this form is fast disappearing and words that used to be divided are often shown as one word.

    eg to-day is now today.
          every-one is now everyone.

Use the hyphen:

- where you change the meaning of the word.

    eg recover – to regain possession or return to health.
    re-cover – to re-cover something such as a chair.
- instead of the word 'to'.
    eg 41–56 Long Road.
- when dividing words at line ends. A hyphen is placed close up to the last letter able to be fitted on the line and the remainder of the word is carried over to the next line. Try to divide between syllables, eg judge-ment, and always make sure at least three letters remain both at the line end and at the beginning of the next line.

The dash –

There are two kinds of dash; the single and the double dash. Use the single dash:

- to show a change of thought.

    eg We went on holiday in August last year – or perhaps it was at the beginning of September.
- to give an explanation.

    eg Susan felt ill after the incident – not surprising in the circumstances.

Use the double dash:

- like brackets, but to give more emphasis.
  eg It was seven in the evening – far too late – when baby James finally went to bed.

The exclamation mark   !

As its name suggests, this mark indicates an exclamation. It is shown at the end of a sentence and its general use is to inject humour.

The question mark   ?

The question mark is shown at the end of a sentence which asks a question. It can also be used to show a query on a date or time etc. An example would be: 'we shall meet at ? on Friday'. The exact time has not yet been decided and will be inserted later on.

Quotation marks   '   '   "   "

These are sometimes called **inverted commas**. Either single or double marks can be used according to preference, although it is more usual to use single nowadays except perhaps in direct speech. If using a quote within a quote, use different marks for each.

> *eg*   "The new book 'Summer in Chicago' is sure to be a hit," said Mr Adams.

The apostrophe   '

Use the apostrophe:

- to show the omission of one or more letters in a word.
  eg There's, isn't, I've.

- to show the possessive form.
  eg Mary's toys, or Molly's dog.

- in names.
  eg O'Toole.

Notes on the use of the apostrophe

1   If the apostrophe is being used to show the possessive use of a plural noun which already ends in 's', the apostrophe will be shown after the 's'.
    eg The lady's shoes. The ladies' shoes.

2   It's and its are often confused. When the word is short for it is, it

should be written with an apostrophe.

eg It's costing far too much money.

When it takes the possessive form meaning belonging to it, no apostrophe is needed.

eg The rabbit had its back to the girl.

Assignment

Read the following letter and correct the mistakes.

Dear Sir,

I wrote you on 24 July asking if you will let me have 100 copies of your new magazine. But I have not heard nothing from you. and I am beginning to get rather worried;

I hope you would not let me down as I had a number of people waiting for copies. Which means my reputation is at stake if I deliver not on time.

If they are not hear by wednesday, I am forced to cancel the order, this will be a pity as I have dealed with you for many years now

Yours faithfully.

See page 172 for suggested answer.

OPEN PUNCTUATION V FULL PUNCTUATION

Open punctuation means to reduce punctuation marks to a minimum. In practice this means omitting punctuation marks:

- after abbreviations

- on envelopes

- in all but the main body of a business letter.

Full punctuation is the rather old fashioned way of punctuating all the above.

OPEN PUNCTUATION	FULL PUNCTUATION
The show starts at 7.30 pm.	The show starts at 7.30 p.m.
30 August 1995.	30th August, 1995.
Joe has an RSA Certificate.	Joe has an R.S.A. Certificate.

Mr A B Smith BSc   Mr. A. B. Smith B.Sc.

Open punctuation is quicker, neater and should always be used in modern, up to date business letters and envelopes.

Assignment

Convert the following examples to open punctuation:

1   Mr. A. Jones, B.A.,
     41, The Highway,
     NORTHDEAN,
     NO4 6AZ

2   The date was the 29th May, 19- -, and the actual time was 9.30 p.m. Mr. B. Salter decided to take his car to the A.B.C. Garage. He thought his car needed some new parts, e.g., brake linings and filters.

See page 172 for suggested answers.

SORTING OUT SENTENCES AND PARAGRAPHS

All text is made up of sentences and paragraphs. You will produce better business letters if you first understand how sentences and paragraphs are constructed.

Sentences

According to *The Oxford Guide to the English Language*, a sentence is a 'set of words making a single complete statement'. To put it another way, a sentence must make sense and it should have a **subject** and a **predicate**.

- The subject is the person or thing being discussed in the sentence. It is normally a noun or a pronoun.

- The predicate says something about the subject and it must contain a verb.

Example

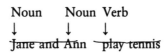

Subjects   Predicate

Sentences can be short or long, although in business letters it is better to make them as short as possible. Try to keep just one idea in each sentence, otherwise your meaning may become unclear.

Paragraphs

A paragraph is one or more sentences grouped around a central theme or subject. When you change your theme or subject, you should begin a new paragraph. Every paragraph should include one sentence (perhaps the opening one) which describes the theme or subject for that whole paragraph. Paragraphs can vary greatly in length, but again in business letters it is best to keep them short – perhaps two or three sentences each.

ADDRESSING IMPORTANT PEOPLE

You may well have to write letters to important people from time to time, and they should be addressed in the appropriate way.

Decorations and qualifications

The dictionary defines 'decorate' as 'to honour a person by giving a medal or badge of honour'. This is indicated by letters after a person's name. Examples of decorations include:

KBE (Knight Commander of the British Empire)

OBE (Officer of the Order of the British Empire)

VC (Victoria Cross).

Decorations are shown before qualifications. If more than one set of letters are to be shown, separate each set with a space. The modern trend is *not* to insert full stops after each letter. Some decorations carry a title: a person with a KBE would be called Sir.

Qualifications and honours show that the person has a degree, or other qualifications, and/or is a member of a professional body. Some qualifications mean that the person can use a title such as Doctor or Professor. Examples include:

BA   (Bachelor of Arts)

BS   (Bachelor of Surgery)

MP (Member of Parliament)

Using the correct form of address

The Queen

It is usual to send a letter for The Queen to 'The Private Secretary to Her Majesty The Queen'. The letter should ask him/her to 'submit for Her Majesty's consideration (or approval)'.

If you do wish to communicate direct with The Queen, the following style should be used:

Beginning	Madam
	With my humble duty
End	I have the honour to remain (or 'to be')
	Madam
	Your Majesty's most humble and obedient
	servant
Envelope	Her Majesty the Queen

Queen Elizabeth The Queen Mother

The same applies as for The Queen, except you would put The Queen Mother.

Other members of the Royal Family

It is usual to write to the Equerry, Private Secretary, or Lady in Waiting of the particular member of the Royal Family.

If you do wish to communicate direct, the following style should be used:

Beginning	Sir (Madam)
End	I have the honour to remain (or 'to be')
	Sir (Madam)
	Your Royal Highness's most humble and
	obedient servant
Envelope	His (Her) Royal Highness
	Followed on the next line by the name

The Prime Minister and other Members of Parliament

Beginning	Dear (Name of Minister)
End	Yours sincerely
Envelope	The Rt Hon (Name) MP (if not member of
	Privy Council, Rt Hon is omitted)

High Court Judge
   Beginning   Dear Judge Jones
   End   Yours sincerely
   Envelope   The Hon Mr (Mrs) Justice Jones

Circuit Judge
   Beginning   Dear Sir/Madam
   End   Yours sincerely
   Envelope   His or Her Honour Judge Jones

The Pope
   Beginning   Your Holiness or Most Holy Father
   End   *If Roman Catholic:*
                      I have the honour to be
                      Your Holiness's most devoted and obedient
                      child (or most humble child)
                      If not Roman Catholic:
                      I have the honour to be (or to remain)
                      Your Holiness's obedient servant
   Envelope   His Holiness
                      The Pope

Archbishops of Canterbury and York
   Beginning   Dear Archbishop
   End   Yours sincerely
   Envelope   The Most Reverend and Right Hon the Lord
                      Archbishop of Canterbury/York

Priest
   Beginning   Dear Father Jones
   End   Yours sincerely
   Envelope   The Reverend Peter Jones

Vicar/Reverend
   Beginning   Dear Mr Jones or Dear Father
                      Jones or Dear Vicar
   End   Yours sincerely
   Envelope   The Reverend Peter Jones

Duke
   Beginning   Dear Duke
   End   Yours sincerely

| Envelope | The Duke of Bath or His Grace the Duke of Bath |

Wife of Duke

Beginning	Dear Duchess
End	Yours sincerely
Envelope	The Duchess of Bath

Marquess, Earl, Viscount and Baron

Beginning	Dear Lord Bath
End	Yours sincerely
Envelope	The Marchioness of Bath
	The Countess of Bath
	The Viscountess of Bath
	The Lady Bath

Baronet

Beginning	Dear Sir Peter
End	Yours sincerely
Envelope	Sir Peter Smith Bt

Knight

Beginning	Dear Sir Peter
End	Yours sincerely
Envelope	Sir Peter Smith KBE

Dame

Beginning	Dear Dame Susan
End	Yours sincerely
Envelope	Dame Susan Moore DBE

CHECKLIST

- Can you give examples of the different parts of speech?
- Have you mastered the use of punctuation?
- Can you explain the difference between open and full punctuation?
- Do your sentences keep to one idea?
- Have you begun a new paragraph for each new topic?
- Do you know how to address important people?

POINTS FOR DISCUSSION

1   Why is the correct use of grammar and punctuation so important in the writing of business letters?

2   Read through a letter you have recently received. Can you find any grammatical, punctuation or spelling mistakes? If you think you can improve on the letter, write it out again.

3   How would you address a letter to your local MP and where would you send it?

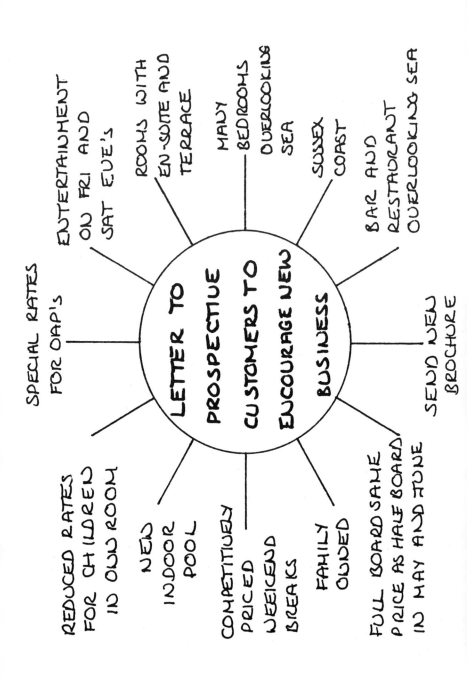

Fig. 4. A spider chart.

3
How to Plan Your Letter

A well planned letter is far more likely to achieve the results you want than one carelessly thrown together in a hurry. In this chapter we will discuss:

- assembling the facts
- deciding what to say
- deciding how to say it
- planning the beginning, middle and end
- writing your first draft.

ASSEMBLING THE FACTS

It is vitally important for a business letter to convey information as accurately and clearly as possible. This means a considerable amount of careful planning in advance.

First of all, the facts need to be assembled. Collect together the relevant files and any other information that is necessary for the composition of your letter. This may involve a certain amount of research, so that you are absolutely sure of your facts before you commit them to paper. Remember that once you have made a statement in a letter it is very difficult to retract that statement at a later date should you find it to be inaccurate for any reason.

DECIDING WHAT TO SAY

What is the **subject** of your letter? **Who** will be reading it? These are two questions you should ask yourself before deciding exactly what to say.

If you have assembled the facts that are to be covered in your letter, you now need to jot those facts down and sort them into a logical order. Once you have done that, go through each point and make sure it is both necessary and accurate.

On the facing page you will see an example of a **spider chart**, showing points to be made in a sales letter from a hotel to prospective customers.

35

The spider chart itself does not follow any sort of order. That order will come later when the points are taken one by one and incorporated into the resulting letter.

DECIDING HOW TO SAY IT

Once again, do stop and think about who you are writing to. For example, it is no use writing a letter full of technical facts and figures if the person at the other end has no technical knowledge whatsoever.

Choice of wording
When thinking about how to word your letter consider the following:

- who the letter is going to
- why the letter is being sent in the first place
- what you hope to achieve by sending the letter.

Once you have answered these questions for yourself you will be in a better position to decide what to say and how to say it.

Things to avoid
Business letters should be brief but very effective and easy to understand. There are a few 'do nots' to bear in mind.

- Do not use slang.
- Do not patronise.
- Do not use flowery language.
- Do not be too formal, or too familiar.
- Do not use words you don't understand.
- Do not demand. It is far better to suggest.

Your letter can, if the situation dictates, be slightly humorous in content. It does not have to read in a 'stuffy' way. Compliments are usually well received, but should only be given if they are deserved.

Try to make your letter a pleasure to read as well as a way of conveying information.

Example
John Price is a rather old fashioned, out of date, sales executive. Steve Roche is younger, more dynamic and a 'fun' person. They work for a fictional drug company called Wonderdrugs Limited. Both men have been asked to write to GPs inviting them to a special lunch to promote

the launching of a new drug called Topturn, which is claimed to be a breakthrough in the treatment of rheumatism.

Both letters give the same information, but in a very different way. See pages 38 and 39.

Assignment

See if you can improve on the wording and paragraphing of this draft letter. It is to a patient from his doctor.

Dear Mr Jones

As you know you came to see me last week. You came to see me for some blood tests. I am writing to tell you the results of the tests. I expect you will be pleased to hear that the blood tests were negative and you do not have anything to worry about.

Let me know if you suffer from further problems in the future.

Yours faithfully

See page 173 for suggested answer.

FINDING THE BEGINNING, MIDDLE AND END

All letters, however, brief, should have a beginning, a middle and an end.

The beginning

The very first paragraph needs to set the scene for the rest of your letter. By the end of that first paragraph the reader should know exactly what the letter is about.

The middle

The remainder of the letter is then sub-divided into more paragraphs, each dealing with a particular topic.

The end

The final paragraph will often sum up the contents of the letter and then end with a request or an assurance, depending on the subject matter.

Keep it short

It is best if both sentences and paragraphs are kept as short as possible in a business letter. No waffle is necessary, just a series of concise paragraphs conveying exactly the right meaning.

WONDERDRUGS LIMITED

51-60 Old Star Street, Pringleton, Sussex PR18 9YN
Telephone: 01243-672368

February 199X

Dear Doctor

As a member of a much valued profession, I should like to formally invite you to a special luncheon we are holding on Monday 3 March 199X at The Ship Hotel in Newtown.

A sherry reception will begin at midday, followed by luncheon at 1.00 pm. A wide choice of menu will be available and all drinks will be provided by our company.

After the luncheon you will be invited to see a short video showing our new product Topturn, which is claimed to be a breakthrough in the treatment of rheumatism. Topturn is shortly to be available in Great Britain, and will, we are sure prove to be of great interest to your for your patients.

We assure you of our best attention at all times and look forward to hearing whether you can spare a few hours of your precious time to join us. Your presence would be greatly appreciated.

Yours truly

John Price
Sales Executive

Notes

1. This letter is very patronising and doctors, in general, do not like to be patronised or made to feel like 'God'.

2. It is far too long and drawn out. Doctors are busy people. They want the facts with no waffle.

3. 'Yours truly' is rather old fashioned now. 'Yours sincerely' is more suitable for a letter such as this.

WONDERDRUGS LIMITED

51-60 Old Star Street, Pringleton, Sussex PR18 9YN
Telephone: 01243-672368

February 199X

Dear Doctor

I am writing to invite you to a special lunch we are holding on Monday 3 March 199X at The Ship Hotel in Newtown.

A sherry reception will begin at midday, followed by lunch at 1.00 pm. A wide choice of menu will be available and all drinks will be provided by our company.

After lunch we invite you to watch a short video showing our new product, Topturn, which is claimed to be a breakthrough in the treatment of rheumatism. Topturn is shortly to be available in Great Britain and will, no doubt, prove to be of great interest to you for your patients.

We hope you will be able to join us and look forward to hearing from you.

Yours sincerely

Steve Roche
Sales Executive

Notes

1. This letter is brief, to the point and easy to read.

2. The doctor can see at a glance what is involved and is much more likely to make a positive decision to attend.

LETTER TO PROSPECTIVE CUSTOMERS TO ENCOURAGE NEW BUSINESS

Date as Postmark

Dear Sir or Madam

We are writing to tell you about our Hotel, which is pleasantly situated on the Sussex coast.

Unlike many other hotels in our area, The Brinks Hotel is family owned. This adds that extra personal touch which is hard to find in the larger 'chains'.

The facilities we offer are far too numerous to mention. We mention just a few below:

- Brand New Indoor Pool
- Bar and Restaurant Overlooking the Sea
- All rooms with en-suite facilities and private terrace
- Many bedrooms overlooking the sea
- Entertainment on Friday and Saturday evenings

We have many special offers available at the present time. We are offering full board for the same price as half board during May and June, and we have competitively priced weekend breaks. Children are well catered for and can be accommodated at reduced rates – even if they share their own room. The older generation are not forgotten with special rates for OAPs.

We are enclosing our latest brochure which gives prices and further information for your guidance. We hope that once you have read through the literature you will decide for yourselves that we are well worth a visit. If this is the case, please give us a ring to discuss your requirements in more detail.

Yours sincerely

WRITING YOUR FIRST DRAFT

Unless you are a very experienced letter writer, it is always best to write out a first draft of your letter before the final copy is prepared.

The first draft can be handwritten or, if you are using a word processor, keyed straight onto your screen and amended as necessary.

Choosing the right salutation and complimentary close

To being with you have to decide on the correct **salutation** (eg Dear Sir) and on the **complimentary close** (eg Yours faithfully). The options to use are shown below:

Beginning:	*End:*
Dear Sir/s or Dear Madam	Yours faithfully
Dear Mr Brown	Yours sincerely
Dear John	Yours sincerely *or* Kind regards Yours sincerely *or* Best wishes Yours sincerely

As we discussed in Chapter 2, it is very important to be aware of the rules of grammar and punctuation when writing a business letter. This is necessary for two reasons:

- Firstly, because your letter is representing the organisation you work for; a badly constructed letter will give a poor impression of your entire organisation.

- The second reason is just as important. Incorrect use of grammar and punctuation can mean a wrong interpretation of what your letter is trying to convey.

Throughout the writing of the letter keep your reader in mind. Make sure you deal with the subject matter in a systematic way and that your sentences and paragraphs 'flow' from one point to another.

Example of a first draft

Opposite is the draft copy of a letter produced from the spider chart on page 36.

Editing your first draft

When you have finished the first draft of your letter, set it aside for as long as you can before reading it through. When you do read it, check for the following:

- Are there any unnecessary words that can be removed?

- Is the letter clear and likely to achieve the desired result?

- Are the relevant facts logically presented?

- Have you included everything the reader will want to know?

- Would *you* react in the way you want your reader to react if *you* were to receive the letter?

Working through this checklist, make changes where necessary. Only when you are absolutely sure that the content of your letter is as perfect as you can possibly make it should you go ahead and produce the final copy.

On the page 43 is the draft letter shown on page 40 with handwritten amendments.

The final copy of this letter is shown on page 44.

CHECKLIST

Have you:
- Assembled all the facts?

- Checked that all the facts are accurate?

- Made notes on what is to be covered in the letter?

- Thought about who the letter is going to?

- Thought about the aim of the letter?

- Chosen your words carefully?

- Divided the letter into a beginning, a middle and an end?

- Made sure you started a new paragraph for each new topic?

DRAFT COPY WITH AMENDMENTS

Date as Postmark

Dear Sir or Madam

We are writing to tell you about our Hotel, which is pleasantly situated on the Sussex coast.

Unlike many other hotels in our area, The Brinks ~~Hotel~~ is family owned. This adds that extra personal touch ~~which~~ *that* is hard to find in the larger 'chains'.

We offer an impressive range of facilities.
~~The facilities we offer are far too numerous to mention. We mention just a few below.~~ *These include :*

lc • Brand New Indoor Pool

lc • Bar and Restaurant Overlooking the Sea

• All ~~rooms~~ *bedrooms* with en-suite facilities and private terrace, *many overlooking the sea*

~~• Many bedrooms overlooking the sea~~

• Entertainment on Friday and Saturday evenings

~~We have many special offers available at the present time,~~ We are offering full board for the same price as half board during May and June *of this year* and we *also* have competitively priced weekend breaks. Children are well catered for and can be accommodated at reduced rates *,* even if they ~~share~~ *have* their own room. The older generation are not forgotten *either,* with special rates for OAPs *all the year round.*

We are enclosing our latest brochure which gives ~~prices and~~ further information *including prices.* ~~for your guidance.~~ *When you have had a chance to look through the brochure we hope* ~~We hope that once you have read through the literature~~ you will decide ~~for yourselves~~ that we are well worth a visit. If ~~this is the case,~~ *so,* please give us a ring to ~~discuss your requirements in more detail.~~ *check availability on your chosen dates.*

Yours ~~sincerely~~ *faithfully*

lc = small letters (lower case)
NP = New paragraph

Tel: 01653 270897

The Brinks Hotel
Enstone Street, Ivytown,
Sussex IV18 1MN

Date as Postmark

Dear Sir or Madam

We are writing to tell you about our Hotel, which is pleasantly situated on the Sussex coast.

Unlike many other hotels in our area, The Brinks is family owned. This adds that extra personal touch that is hard to find in the larger 'chains'.

We offer an impressive range of facilities. These include:

* Brand new indoor pool

* Bar and restaurant overlooking the sea

* All bedrooms with en-suite facilities and private terrace, many overlooking the sea

* Entertainment on Friday and Saturday evenings

We are offering full board for the same price as half board during May and June of this year, and we also have competitively priced weekend breaks. Children are well catered for and can be accommodated at reduced rates, even if they have their own room. The older generation are not forgotten either, with special rates for OAPs all the year round.

We are enclosing our latest brochure which gives you further information, including prices.

When you have had a chance to look through the brochure we hope you will decide that we are well worth a visit. If so, please give us a ring to check availability on your chosen dates.

Yours faithfully

- Kept sentences and paragraphs as short as possible?

- Written a first draft?

- Amended the first draft where necessary?

- Prepared the final copy?

- Made sure your letter is a pleasure to read?

POINTS FOR DISCUSSION

1. What are the main aims of a business letter?

2. In what circumstances do you think a business letter should be very formal?

3. You have been asked to send a letter to an unsuccessful candidate for a job interview. Work out a rough draft of this letter, bearing in mind that tact and gentle treatment are necessary.

4
How to Present Your letter

USING THE COMPANY LETTERHEAD

Almost all companies and organisations have their own printed letterhead to be used for all business letters. These letterheads are often used for other documents, too, such as memos, invoices, and statements.

A printed letterhead should contain the name of the company, its address and telephone number. Where applicable, other details such as telex number, fax number, names of directors, company registration number and VAT number can also be shown.

Two examples of printed letterheads are shown below:

Softy Fabrics
3 Denmark Rise, Newtown NE3 1YH
Tel: 3468 714856 Fax: 3468 718921

Your Ref
Our Ref

The Animal Kingdom
Bruin Street
Newtown NE10 0PY   Tel: 3691 279017

DESIGNING YOUR OWN LETTERHEAD

If you work for a company you will probably use their letterhead without giving the matter much thought. If you ever need to design your own letterhead, however, you will soon see that quite a lot of thought has to be put into the initial design and layout.

Do you sometimes receive letters that look dull and uninteresting, all because of their unimaginative letterheads? What sort of impression does that give of the company? It certainly does not suggest a dynamic organisation. In these days of fierce competition, every extra helps, and an eye-catching letterhead gets you off to a good start.

What information to show

First of all, think about what you must show on your letterhead. This will depend on the type of business in which you are involved. For example, if your business is a limited company then you must show the full name of the company, the names of all the directors, the company registration number, the place of company registration, and the address of the company's registered office. If it is not a limited company then the content of the letterhead is entirely up to you.

Any letterhead that you design should:

- be clear and easy to read

- show the name, address and telephone number of your company

- show any fax number, or telex number

- give any other information that would be helpful to the recipient of the letter.

Using a logo

Many companies adopt a **logo** to be shown on all their headed paper. This is often a picture or symbol that can easily be related to the company in question. Logos can be a very effective way of advertising your company, particularly if you keep the same logo on all business documents as well as in newspaper advertising and promotion campaigns. You may need to consult a designer on the logo best for you and although this could cost you hard earned money, the chances are that a professional logo will pay off in the end. Indeed, your company could eventually be recognised more by its logo than its name.

Using colour

Your letterhead can be printed out in bold type and/or in colour and you should aim to make it look as spectacular as you possibly can. After all, the more attractive you make it, the more impressed the recipients of your letters will be.

Page size and layout

Most companies use A4 paper (297 x 210 mm) even for their short business letters as it is cheaper and more convenient to keep to one size of paper. An A4 sheet also gives a lot more scope for your letterhead than A5 (210 x 148 mm), particularly if you need to display information such as company registration address and number and the names of directors. If this is the case, the best plan is to set the company address, telephone number and so on at the top of the letterhead and directors' names and company registration details at the bottom. Otherwise, you would be in a situation where the heading is so long that the letter starts halfway down the page!

To sum up, besides containing valuable information, letterheads must be clear, eye catching and generally give a good impression of the company or organisation they are representing.

LAYING OUT YOUR LETTER

The layout of a business letter has become far simpler in recent years. There are still certain guidelines to follow, but with the use of **open punctuation** (see Chapter 3) and the **fully blocked layout**, business letters can be quickly and easily prepared.

By the term fully blocked we mean that every line begins at the left margin. The old fashioned way of indenting paragraphs and centring headings in business letters, with punctuation scattered about like confetti, takes extra time and is just not necessary.

When thinking about the presentation of your letter, remember:

- Keep to the fully blocked layout with open punctuation.
- If possible, line up your left margin with the left edge of your letterhead.
- Address your letter to an individual if you have a personal name to use.
- Check for errors when you get to the end of your letter.
- Make sure that the letter is the best you can produce.

Example of fully blocked letter

An example of a fully blocked letter with open punctuation is shown on p50.

The numbers shown at the left-hand side of the example are explained below:

1. The company printed heading (explained page 46).

2. References. The words 'Your Ref' will only be inserted if previous correspondence from the recipient shows a reference. 'Our Ref' usually consists of the initials of the sender and of the typist/word processor operator. A file number can be added.

3. Date. A letter must always have a date and there is no need to put 'th' or 'st' after the number, eg 5 May 199X, not 5th May 199X.

4. Any special message. Eg 'For the Attention of', 'Urgent', or 'Confidential'.

5. Inside name and address. This is the name and address of the person to whom the letter is being sent. Use a separate line for each part of the address. The post town should be in capital letters.

6. The salutation or greeting. (See Chapter 2 for information on addressing important people.) It is far better, if possible, to start your letter with a personal name, for example Dear Mr Bloggs, rather than Dear Sir.

7. Subject heading.

8. Main body of the letter, sub-divided into paragraphs.

9. Complimentary close. This should be in accordance with the salutation. Examples are:

    Dear Sir/Madam   Yours faithfully
    Dear Mr Smith   Yours sincerely

    Remember that 'faithfully' and 'sincerely' do *not* begin with capital letters.

10. The name of the company may be shown immediately under the complimentary close.

11. The name of the sender and his/her designation or position.

12. The enclosure mark. This indicates that something is to be sent with the letter. Some companies have their own method of showing an enclosure, such as a sticky label.

1. ## Seaside Travel Ltd
   65-70 Sunny Street, Littletown L12 7DY
   Tel No. 7896 2541 Fax No 7896 5698

2. Your Ref SMH/CWJ
   Our Ref JAP/CD
   x
3. 16 September 19- -
   x
4. FOR THE ATTENTION OF MR A BAKER
   x
5. Baker & Company Ltd
   63 The Walk
   LITTLETOWN
   LI25 7NK
   x
6. Dear Sir
   x
7. <u>Travel Bag Promotion</u>
   x
   You will remember that we wrote to you back in June, asking for a Quotation for you to supply approximately 1,000 of your best quality travel bags for our Christmas promotion. By return you kindly sent us a sample and a price of £5.00 per bag.
   x
8. We are now in a position to place a definite order with you for 1,250 bags. We hope the extra number will not be a problem. From the suggested colours we have decided on Burgundy. We leave the actual choice of contents to yourselves, so long as we keep within our £5.00 budget per bag. Your colour chart is enclosed.
   x
   We should like delivery by mid-November, and we look forward to your confirmation that this will be possible.
   x
9. Yours faithfully
10. SEASIDE TRAVEL LTD
    x
    x
    x
    x
11. Jane A Prior (Ms)
    DIRECTOR
    x
12. enc

Fig. 5. A fully blocked letter using open punctuation.
NOTE: x = one clear line of space.

50

Writing a circular letter

Occasionally a company needs to send a large number of identical letters, for example advertising a new product or inviting people to attend a special exhibition. What is known as a **circular** letter can be used for this purpose. It is so called because it is 'circulated' (distributed) to many people.

All copies of the letter will be identical rather than personalised. The date is often shown as 'Date as Postmark', meaning that the franking on the envelope will show when it was posted, or alternatively the month and year can be used. This gives more flexibility in sending the letter out over a period of time. There does not have to be an inside name and address, although sometimes one is inserted to make the letter seem more personalised.

Tear off slips

Many circular letters end with a tear off portion. The recipient, should he or she wish, tears this off, fills it in and returns it to the company. The tear off slip should finish approximately 25 mm (1″) from the bottom of the page.

Planning a circular letter

If you plan to send a circular letter:

- Prepare it well, so that it is less likely to be thought of as 'junk mail'.

- Make sure the tear off portion is easy to understand, otherwise the wrong information may be returned to you.

- Use a good quality photocopier or printer for the copies. An old photocopier with 'splodges' will not create a good impression.

- Consider using the mail merge facility on your word processor – if you have one – so that the letter can become more personalised (see Chapter 5).

Example

An example of a circular letter is shown on page 52.

Assignments

1. You are Mrs B Smith of 21 Orbit Road, London W8 9RT. You have received a copy of the circular letter with tear off slip on page 52. You have not paid the balance of your holiday money because you have been in hospital. You are now home but will be unable to

Seaside Travel Ltd

65-70 Sunny Street, Littletown L12 7DY
Tel No. 7896 2541 Fax No 7896 5698

December 19- -

Dear Sir/Madam

HOLIDAY IN PORTUGAL – MARCH 19 - -

With regard to your booking for the above holiday, we are writing to ask you to send us your final payment without delay.

When you gave us your deposit, we stated clearly that the balance was to be paid by 15 November. This deadline has now passed and we have not received any money from you.

Would you kindly fill in the tear off slip at the bottom of this letter and return it to us with your payment. If, for any reason, you are unable to take the holiday, we would still ask you to return the slip. No refunds will be given for deposit money paid.

Yours faithfully
SEASIDE TRAVEL LTD

Jane A Prior (Ms)
DIRECTOR

- -

*I enclose the balance of my holiday payment as requested.
*I wish to cancel my holiday booking.

Name .... *Mr/Mrs/Miss/Ms

Address...

....

*Delete as applicable

Fig. 6. Example of a circular letter.

52

travel abroad in March. Write to Seaside Travel and say that you are enclosing a letter from your doctor. Ask whether you will be able to get your deposit money back in view of the special circumstances. Date the letter 2 January 199X.

2. Acting as Jane Prior of Seaside Travel, reply to Mrs Smith's letter suggesting that she should send her letter to the insurance company mentioned on her travel documents, to see if they can arrange a refund of her deposit. Say that you are very sorry to hear of her problems and hope that she will be able to take a holiday at a later date. Date the letter 9 January 199X.

See page 174/175 for suggested answers.

HEADING UP A CONTINUATION SHEET

If your business letter continues onto a second or subsequent page, a continuation sheet will need to be prepared. Plain, rather than headed paper is normally used for this.

---

x
x
x
2
x
24 September 19 - -
x
Mrs J Smith
x
x
x
I wish you a very speedy recovery from your illness and hope that very soon you will be feeling fully fit once more. Please let me know if there is anything you need.
x
Yours sincerely

Note: x = one clear line of space. Leave *at least* three lines clear at the top of the continuation page and approximately 25 mm of space at the bottom of the previous page. Remember that if using a word processing program you will probably have 25 mm automatically set at the top of each page, in which case you would not leave an extra three lines.

Seaside Travel Ltd

65-70 Sunny Street, Littletown LI12 7DY
Tel No. 7896 2541 Fax No 7896 5698

Our Ref JAP/CD

7 October 199X

Mrs A Stephens
68 The Walk
Winchmore Hill
LONDON
N21 8DY

Dear Mrs Stephens

Thank you very much for your letter of 1 October enquiring about holidays in Devon.

Unfortunately, we do not deal specifically with the walking type of holiday you mention. We do, however, know of a company in London who specialise in walking holidays. We are therefore passing your letter to them and we are sure they will be in contact with you in the near future.

Thank you for your interest in Seaside Travel and we hope to be of service to you in the future.

Yours sincerely
SEASIDE TRAVEL LTD

Jane A Prior (Ms)
DIRECTOR

Copy to Mr A Plummer Happy Walking Holidays Ltd

Fig. 7. A fully blocked letter with a marked copy for another person.

There is no need to put a catchphrase such as 'pto' (please turn over) or 'contd' at the end of the first page. Simply go onto the second page and show the page number, the date, and the name (or company name if no personal name) of the person the letter is going to, as shown on page 53.

TAKING A COPY

A copy is taken of most business letters for the company file. This can be a carbon copy or a photocopy.

- Carbons are messy and take time.

- A photocopy is much easier and many companies rely on their photocopier for all their copies.

When using a computer to prepare a letter, the file copy can either be stored on disk where it can be accessed if necessary, or two printed copies can be made at the time the letter is typed.

If a copy is to be sent to someone outside the company this is usually shown at the end of the letter (see page 54). Very occasionally the sender will not wish the recipient to know they are sending a copy to someone else. In this case the letters 'bc' (blind copy) followed by the name of the person receiving the copy, is marked at the bottom of the company file copy only.

PROVIDING AN ENVELOPE OR LABEL

Unless a letter is being sent by fax, an envelope or label will usually need to be prepared.

Positioning the name and address

Many companies use window envelopes, in which case the name and address on the letter must be placed in a set place. If the letter is folded correctly the address will show through the window.

If a normal (not window) envelope of any size is to be prepared, a good rule to remember is to start the address half way down and one third across. Set out the address exactly the same as on the letter.

Positioning special messages

If an Attention line or special message, eg Confidential, is shown on the letter, always include it on the envelope or label too. An example is on page 56.

CONFIDENTIAL

Mr P Clark
Chambers & Clark Ltd
61 The Street
LITTLETOWN
LI2 8LF

Using address labels

Labels are normally produced on long strips or sheets and then peeled off and stuck on envelopes as required. They are very fiddly and do not look as personalised as an envelope with the address typed directly onto it, but they are quick and easy to use.

CHECKLIST

- Have you thought about the letterhead?

- Do you know the parts of a business letter?

- Are you able to display a circular letter effectively?

- Can you head up a continuation sheet?

- Does your finished letter look impressive?

- Have you taken a copy?

- Have you produced an envelope or label to go with your letter?

POINTS FOR DISCUSSION

1. Why is the design of a letterhead so important?

2. What do the terms 'fully blocked' and 'open punctuation' mean?

3. Without referring to this book, make a rough list of the parts of a typical business letter. When you have finished, use the book to check and see if you remembered them all.

5
How to Use
Word Processing Systems

INTRODUCING WORD PROCESSING

The term 'word processing' means exactly what it says – the processing of words or text. Word processing is normally carried out on a computer using a word processing program, of which there are many. Computers are also, of course, capable of performing many other functions depending on which program is being used at the time.

Hardware and software

You may have heard the terms **hardware** and **software**. Hardware refers to the parts that make up the actual computer. The programs that run on the computer are known as software. The hardware is no use without the software, and vice versa.

Operating a system

The person who keys text into a computer using a word processing program is often called a word processing operator. The computer will only do what the operator tells it. It does not work all on its own as some people seem to think!

While the text is being keyed in it can be amended as necessary. When the keying in is finished the document (a 'hard copy') can be printed out and/or stored for future use. At any time in the future the text can be amended or updated by calling back the relevant document onto your screen.

It should be noted that there is also a range of machines available which are actually called word processors. Unlike computers, these machines will normally only operate as word processors and will not perform any other functions.

Word processing programs make normal typing skills much easier to perform. There are a few exceptions such as preparing envelopes and filling in forms, but generally speaking word processing has taken the hard graft out of preparing documents in the modern office.

LOOKING AT THE ADVANTAGES

So why is it so much quicker and easier to use a computer and a word processing program rather than a conventional typewriter? What special functions can most word processing programs perform?

They can:

- Show text on a screen.

- Store text.

- Delete or add text.

- Re-arrange text.

- Correct text.

- Justify text (so that the left and right margins are equal).

- Centre text (particularly useful for headings).

- Underline and embolden text.

- Check the spelling of text.

- Add headers and footers to text (to give page numbers and other information at the top and bottom of the page).

- Display text in columns.

- Change line spacing and pitch size.

- Merge names and addresses with standard letters.

Obviously all these important functions can save the operator a good deal of time. It should also, in theory, be possible to produce a perfect document every time, although the machine will only do what the operator asks of it, so mistakes can still creep in through human error.

The unique feature of a word processing program compared to a typewriter with regard to business letters, is that your letter can be drafted, amended, and only printed out when you are perfectly happy with its layout and presentation. With a typewriter this could mean typing out the same letter several times!

Once you are happy with your letter and have printed out the top copy, you can either print another copy for the files, and/or store the document to be reproduced or referred to at a later date.

Although many companies do still rely on a paper filing system, computer storage and retrieval is becoming more and more widespread; it will probably be the only way that documents are stored in the future.

PREPARING STANDARD LETTERS AND PARAGRAPHS

A standard letter is one sent out to many different people, containing the same basic information. Many companies now keep a selection of standard letters stored on their computer for use as required. This saves a great deal of time.

Standard letters can take several forms. They may be straightforward letters, beginning with an impersonal name like 'Dear Customer', or space may be left for the insertion of individual names and addresses.

When using a word processing program, it is an easy task to fill in any necessary information and then to print out a perfect top copy of your business letter every time.

An example of a standard letter follows:

ANYONE'S BANK

The Street, Churchtown
Sussex BN26 7YG

Date as Postmark

Dear Customer

It has come to our notice that once again, your account has become overdrawn. A sum of £20.00 has been debited from your account to deal with the administrative costs in connection with this unauthorised overdraft.

Would you please make sure that sufficient funds are transferred to your account at the very earliest opportunity.

Yours faithfully

James A Butler
MANAGER

Fig. 8. Standard letter with no space left for name and address.

Standard paragraphs can also be stored to be used in business letters. A number of commonly used paragraphs can be prepared and stored as say, 'Para 1, Para 2'. It is sometimes possible to compile whole letters just by using the standard paragraphs, but care should be taken to make sure that the paragraphs have been used in the correct way, otherwise your letter might not make sense and then nothing will have been gained by their use.

Example

Para 1   Thank you for your letter of . . . . The matter you mention is receiving our attention.

Para 2   Thank you for your order which is greatly appreciated.

Para 3   We shall be contacting you again shortly with a view to arranging a meeting to discuss this matter in more detail.

Para 4   Unfortunately we do not have the goods you require in stock at the present time, but we are expecting them in during the next few days. We hope this will be soon enough for you.

Para 5   The goods you require will be sent by British Rail and should arrive within the next week.

Para 6   Please let us know if we can be of any further service.

Para 7   Yours sincerely [or] Yours faithfully.

Samuel Price
Director

These paragraphs are to be used in the following three letters as demonstrated on pages 62, 63 and 64.

USING THE MAIL MERGE FACILITY

A 'mail merge' means combining two files to produce several different documents.

- The first file is rather like a card index system found in the office, each card containing information. This file is often called the database.

THE NUT AND BOLT EMPORIUM

James Street, Littletown LI2 9HG

Tel No: 1234-8970 Fax No: 1234-9185

21 May 199X

Mr Russell Scott
Scott Electrics Ltd
234 Adam Street
LITTLETOWN
LI1 9YN

Dear Mr Scott

Thank you for your order which is greatly appreciated.

The goods you require will be sent by British Rail and should arrive within the next week.

Please let us know if we can be of any further service.

Yours sincerely

Samuel Price
Director

Fig 9. Letter 1 – using Para 2, 5, 6 and 7.

THE NUT AND BOLT EMPORIUM

James Street, Littletown LI2 9HG

Tel No: 1234-8970 Fax No: 1234-9185

3 June 199X

Reynolds and Smith
56 The Broadway
LITTLETOWN
LI1 8YN

Dear Sirs

Thank you for your letter of 28 May 199X. The matter you mention
is receiving our attention.

We shall be contacting you again shortly with a view to arranging a
meeting to discuss this matter in more detail.

Yours faithfully

Samuel Price
Director

Fig. 10. Wordprocessing letter 2 – using Para 1, 3 and 7.

THE NUT AND BOLT EMPORIUM

James Street, Littletown LI2 9HG

Tel No: 1234-8970 Fax No: 1234-9185

4 July 199X

Mr S Steele
Steele Wood Co
45 Green Lane
LITTLETOWN
LI6 5YH

Dear Mr Steele

Thank you for your order which is greatly appreciated.

Unfortunately we do not have the goods you require in stock at the present time, but we are expecting them in during the next few days. We hope this will be soon enough for you.

Please let us know if we can be of any further service.

Yours sincerely

Samuel Price
Director

Fig 11. Word processing, letter 3 – using Para 2, 4, 6, and 7.

- The second file is any form of document which contains codes for the various pieces of information to be inserted during the merge.

In its simplified form the database could be a list of names and addresses and the second document a letter.

An example of how this works is shown below and on pages 66 and 67.

Record 1 Mr A Smith

56 South Street
BRIDGENORTH
Sussex
BR10 6YH

Mr Smith

Record 2 Mrs C Jones

89 Ship Street
BRIDGENORTH
Sussex
BR10 4NG

Mrs Jones

Record 3 Mr and Mrs P Stiles

12 Toneberry Terrace
BRIDGENORTH
Sussex
BR10 90Y

Mr and Mrs Stiles

DECIDING PRINT QUALITY

Using a word processing program for your business letters does not guarantee more professional results than could be achieved by using a good quality electronic typewriter. Firstly, the keying in has to be accurate. Secondly, the presentation has to be effective and thirdly, the quality of the printing can enhance or detract from the finished appearance.

ANYONE'S BANK

The Street, Churchtown
Sussex BN26 7YG

[Date – most programs can automatically insert the date]

[Code for name]
[Code for address]

Dear [Code for salutation]

It has come to our notice that once again, your account has
become overdrawn. A sum of £20.00 has been debited from
your account to deal with the administrative costs in
connection with this unauthorised overdraft.

Would you please make sure that sufficient funds are
transferred to your account at the very earliest opportunity.

Yours sincerely

James A Butler
MANAGER

Fig 12. The standard letter taken from page 60 with
codes inserted for 'merging'.

ANYONE'S BANK

The Street, Churchtown
Sussex BN26 7YG

25 September 199X

Mr and Mrs P Stiles
12 Toneberry Terrace
BRIDGENORTH
Sussex
BR10 90Y

Dear Mr and Mrs Stiles

It has come to our notice that once again, your account has become overdrawn. A sum of £20.00 has been debited from your account to deal with the administrative costs in connection with this unauthorised overdraft.

Would you please make sure that sufficient funds are transferred to your account at the very earliest opportunity.

Yours faithfully

James A Butler
MANAGER

Fig. 13. An example of a finished letter using the mail merge facility.

The most popular printers in current use are:

- dot matrix
- ink jet
- laser.

Dot matrix printers

This type of printer operates by forming dots using a series of tiny needles. Generally speaking, the more needles the better the printed result. Early dot matrix printers gave very poor results, but they have improved dramatically in recent years. A good quality dot matrix printer should be adequate for most business uses.

An electronic typewriter with a carbon ribbon will still have the edge on most dot matrix printers, however, so if quality, rather than cost, is of paramount importance then one of the other two options may be a better choice.

Ink jet printers

Ink jet printers throw tiny jets of ink rapidly on to the paper. They give a more professional look than dot matrix printers. Like dot matrix, ink jet printers have improved over the years, particularly in terms of their running costs, which used to be very expensive.

Ink jet printers are ideal for any small business user who wants to produce very good quality copy, reasonably cheaply and quickly.

Laser printers

Top of the popular printer range is the laser printer. This is very similar in appearance and operation to a photocopier. It is better and faster than either the dot matrix or the ink jet and can handle vast quantities of paper in no time at all, producing top class copies. Unfortunately it is usually the most expensive of the three types to buy. Costs have come down recently, however, and many companies find that the laser printer is well worth the extra capital outlay and running costs.

CHECKLIST

- Can you explain what the terms hardware and software mean?

- Have you tried using a word processing program on a computer?

- Can you think of all the major tasks that a word processing program can perform?

• Do you understand the uses of standard letters and paragraphs?

• When do you think you could make use of the mail merge facility?

• Are you familiar with the different types of printers available?

POINTS FOR DISCUSSION

1. You are working as a sales administrator in a company specialising in word processing programs. Prepare a standard letter to send out to potential customers persuading them that your program 'Wordmagic' is the one for them.

2. The company you work for has a number of fairly new electronic typewriters in use. The secretaries and office staff would like these replaced with computers and a word processing package, but the boss needs convincing. Working as the managing director's personal assistant write a letter to your local computer company asking them if they can come down to your company to give a talk and demonstration on word processing applications.

3. Prepare a report on the different types of printers available. List the advantages and disadvantages of each. Send the report with a covering letter to your friend who has a business in London and needs a new printer. His name and business address is: Mr A Wright, Wright Enterprises, 65 Wentworth Street, LITTLETOWN LI1 6BF.

Check that your letter is not:

unnecessary	unprepared	full of errors
ambiguous	poorly presented	wrongly addressed
boring	badly worded	wordy
patronising	'flowery'	inaccurate
muddled	hard to understand	inconclusive
too long	badly punctuated	hard to read
rude	a mess	a disgrace

Make sure that your letter is:

accurate	well presented	error free
explicit	practical	respectful
courteous	informative	polite
readable	grammatically correct	well prepared
organised	properly addressed	understandable
factual	achieving its aim	well punctuated
paragraphed	free of errors	logical
simple	to the point	jargon free
impressive	enlightening	complimentary

Make YOUR letters a pleasure to read!

Taking a long, hard look at your letter.

6
Letters to
Customers and Suppliers

INTRODUCTION

Writing to customers and suppliers forms an essential part of the everyday life of most organisations.

Potential customers need to be nurtured and persuaded to buy from your company. Existing customers need to be looked after too, otherwise they might decide to buy elsewhere.

Contact with suppliers is also important. You need to know that the goods you are buying are at a competitive price, and a good business relationship between yourselves and your suppliers will pay dividends.

Using the right approach to customers and suppliers

When writing to customers and suppliers remember the following:

- Always use a polite tone even if you or your customer/supplier has a complaint to make.
- Make the letter brief but ensure that all relevant information is included.
- Ask any necessary questions.
- Provide any necessary answers.
- Never make a promise that you cannot keep.
- Aim to achieve and maintain a good business relationship.

The sample letters

The sample letters in this chapter illustrate the following:

Letter	Pages	Letter	Pages
Asking for information	72-73	Following up an enquiry	74-75
Sending a quotation	76-77	Ordering some goods	78-79
Clarifying an order	80-81	Accepting an order	82-83

Super Toys Ltd
Chattisfield Road, NEWTON NE12 0LD
Tel No: 2567 591048 Fax No: 2567 651987

24 January 199X

Mr Brian Fuller
Softy Fabrics
3 Denmark Rise
NEWTON
NE3 1YH

Dear Mr Fuller

I have been asked by John Updike to write to you to ask you if you could supply us with some of the special white fur you supplied us with last year. I can't remember what he said it was called, but no doubt you will remember anyway.

I think we will want about 5,000 metres if the price is right. If we needed more, would we be able to have it?

Can you let us know as soon as you possibly can whether or not we can have it. If we can't Mr Updike will go elsewhere. Hope you are keeping well.

Yours faithfully

Chris Masters

Asking for information (1)
1. The letter is badly worded, and does not give enough information.
2. The ending of 'hope you are keeping well' is totally irrelevant and should be a new paragraph anyway.
3. A letter that begins Dear Mr/Mrs should end with Yours sincerely, not faithfully. Chris should have also said who he is under his name.
4. Upon receiving this letter Softy Fabrics would have no option but to write back asking for more details.

Super Toys Ltd

Chattisfield Road, NEWTON NE12 0LD
Tel No: 2567 591048 Fax No: 2567 651987

24 January 199X

Mr Brian Fuller
Softy Fabrics
3 Denmark Rise
NEWTON
NE3 1YH

Dear Mr Fuller

We would like to purchase a further quantity of the white fur you supplied us with last year, subject to a satisfactory price being agreed. The Order Number for this was 34017 and the fur was called 'Sheer Delight'.

We require approximately 5,000 metres of the fur, although we need to know whether we would be able to obtain more if necessary. The price last year was £2.00 a metre. Would you be able to offer us the same terms?

Perhaps you would be kind enough to let us know if you can supply us with this fur, how much is available, the price per metre, and when delivery would take place.

Yours sincerely

Sue Chapman (Miss)
Management Trainee

Asking for information (2)

1. All the necessary information is given, including the Order Number and name of the fur, which Sue has bothered to find out.

2. The summing up in the last paragraph adds clarity and should prompt a speedy reply.

Softy Fabrics

3 Denmark Rise · Newtown · NE3 1YH
Tel: 3468 714856 · Fax: 3468 718921

Your Ref
Our Ref BF/SS

30 Jan 199X

Miss Sue Chapman
Super Toys Ltd
Chattisfield Road
NEWTOWN NE12 OLD

Dear Madam

Thank you for your letter of 24 Jan 199X. We can
certainly supply the fur fabric you require. The
price will be the same as before, ie £2.00 a
metre and delivery can be next week if you
require. We have plenty of stock so we could
repeat the order if necessary. Please let us know
if this is acceptable to you.

Yours faithfully

Sara Smythe (Ms)

Following up an enquiry (1)

1. This letter is poorly displayed. The month should be shown in full. The postcode needs a separate line. The letter is addressed to Miss Sue Chapman, so it should begin with 'Dear Miss Chapman'. The subject matter has not been divided into paragraphs. Sara has not shown her job title.

2. Insufficient information has been given for the letter to be effective.

Softy Fabrics

3 Denmark Rise · Newtown · NE3 1YH
Tel: 3468 714856 · Fax: 3468 718921

Your Ref
Our Ref BF/SP

30 January 199X

Miss Sue Chapman
Super Toys Ltd
Chattisfield Road
NEWTOWN
NE12 OLD

Dear Miss Chapman

With reference to your letter of 24 March,
addressed to Brian Fuller, we can certainly supply
you with the fur fabric 'Sheer Delight' in white.

As you are a very good customer, we are prepared
to process your order of 5,000 metres at the old
price of £2.00 a metre. We would deliver next week
at any time to suit yourselves.

We hold considerable stocks of this particular
range, so further orders should not be a problem.

Perhaps you would be kind enough to let us know
the day and time you would like delivery to take
place.

Yours sincerely

Simon Palmer
Management Trainee

Following up an enquiry (2)

1. Simon has been crafty and worded the letter as though the order has already been placed, rather that just thought about.

2. This approach is friendly, easy to read and fully informative.

Super Toys Ltd

Chattisfield Road, NEWTON NE12 0LD
Tel No: 2567 591048 Fax No: 2567 651987

3 February 199X

Mr Nigel Flack
The Animal Kingdom
Bruin Street
NEWTOWN
NE10 0PY

Dear Mr Flack

Further to your telephone conversation with Miss Sue Chapman, I am giving a quotation below for your animals:

120 Hedgehogs, 50 cm in size @ £1.50 each
200 Giraffes, 200 cm in size @ £1.50 each
400 Mice, 50 cm in size @ £1.20 each
500 Blue 'Bugs', 25 cm in size @ 50p each

Please let us know if you wish to place an order with us.

Yours sincerely

Chris Masters
Management Trainee

Sending a quotation (1)

1. Usually any form of quotation is accompanied by some standard terms and conditions. These are not mentioned and no quotation number has been given. Similarly a delivery date is not shown.

2. The wording of the letter, especially the opening and closing paragraphs, is poor in terms of grammar and content.

Super Toys Ltd

Chattisfield Road, NEWTON NE12 0LD
Tel No: 2567 591048 Fax No: 2567 651987

3 February 199X

Mr Nigel Flack
The Animal Kingdom
Bruin Street
NEWTOWN
NE10 0PY

Dear Mr Flack

Further to our telephone conversation the other day, I am giving a quotation below for the soft toys you require:

Quotation Number 1437

120 Hedgehogs, 50 cm in size @ £1.50 each
200 Giraffes, 200 cm in size @ £1.50 each
400 Mice, 50 cm in size @ £1.20 each
500 Blue 'Bugs', 25 cm in size @ 50p each

Terms of Settlement: 30 days. Conditions printed overleaf. Delivery within 2 weeks.

We trust this quotation will meet with your satisfaction and look forward to hearing from you.

Yours sincerely

Sue Chapman (Miss)
Management Trainee

Sending a quotation (2)

Sue has spelt out the information in a concise way. The Quotation Number has been given for reference. Terms and conditions are included.

The Animal Kingdom

Bruin Street, Newtown, NE10 0PY
Telephone: 3691 279017

19 February 199X

Miss Sue Chapman
Super Toys Ltd
Chattisfield Road
NEWTOWN
NE12 OLD

Dear Miss Chapman

Thank you for your Quotation letter of 3 February. We would like to order all the things you quote for. We will pay you cash on delivery and would like you to deliver them as soon as possible.

Yours sincerely

Nigel Flack

Ordering some goods (1)

1. Nigel has prepared this letter in a hurry. He wants to get the order in without the bother of itemising all the items. Jenny, his partner is not happy with his efforts, however, and has asked him if he can do the letter again, giving full details of the items to be ordered. No Order Number has been given.

2. In real life no self respecting company would dispatch an order on the instructions of a vague letter such as this. Super Toys would be forced to write back for clarification.

The Animal Kingdom

Bruin Street, Newtown, NE10 0PY
Telephone: 3691 279017

19 February 199X

Miss Sue Chapman
Super Toys Ltd
Chattisfield Road
NEWTOWN
NE12 OLD

Dear Miss Chapman

Further to your letter of 3 February, I am pleased to confirm our Order number 346 for the following goods, as per your Quotation number 1437.

120 Hedgehogs, 50 cm in size @ £1.00 each
200 Giraffes, 200 cm in size @ £1.50 each
400 Mice, 50 cm in size @ £1.20 each
500 Blue 'Bugs', 25 cm in size @ 50p each

We should like these goods as soon as possible and we will pay cash on delivery.

Yours sincerely

Nigel Flack
Partner

Ordering some goods (2)

1. Full order details are now included. The letter should be sufficient for Super Toys to process the order.

2. There is one problem. Nigel has listed the Hedgehogs as costing £1.00 each, when in fact they were quoted at £1.50. The next letter will clarify this error.

Super Toys Ltd

Chattisfield Road, NEWTON NE12 0LD
Tel No: 2567 591048 Fax No: 2567 651987

22 February 199X

Mr Nigel Flack
The Animal Kingdom
Bruin Street
NEWTOWN
NE10 0PY

Dear Mr Flack

Thank you for your order of 19 February, but I'm afraid you've got it wrong. The Hedgehogs cost £1.50 not £1.00, so do you still want them or not?

Perhaps you could let us know as soon as possible, as you are holding up the order.

Yours sincerely

Chris Masters
Management Trainee

Clarifying an order (1)

As you will see by now, Chris will not win an award for tact and good use of the English language! His tone is wrong – almost rude, and he is overusing abbreviated words.

Super Toys Ltd

Chattisfield Road, NEWTON NE12 0LD
Tel No: 2567 591048 Fax No: 2567 651987

22 February 199X

Mr Nigel Flack
The Animal Kingdom
Bruin Street
NEWTOWN
NE10 0PY

Dear Mr Flack

Thank you very much for your Order, number 346, which we received this morning.

At the moment we are unable to supply the goods as there seems to be a discrepancy over the price of the Hedgehogs. Our Quotation 1437 states the cost per Hedgehog to be £1.50, whereas you state £1.00 on your Order. Our Quotation is the correct price and we wonder if you would be kind enough to telephone us, at your convenience, to clarify this matter.

We look forward to hearing from you.

Yours sincerely

Sue Chapman (Miss)
Management Trainee

Clarifying an order (2)

1. Sue has explained the problem in a polite way.

2. A telephone call is a good suggestion to make in order to clarify a problem such as this. The telephone call can then be followed up by a letter from Super Toys accepting the order, but while this letter is working its way across to Animal Kingdom the goods can be prepared for delivery. The Order number and the Quotation number are both quoted to save any misunderstandings.

Super Toys Ltd

Chattisfield Road, NEWTON NE12 0LD
Tel No: 2567 591048 Fax No: 2567 651987

25 February 199X

Mr Nigel Flack
The Animal Kingdom
Bruin Street
NEWTOWN
NE10 0PY

Dear Mr Flack

Thanks for your tel call yesterday. Glad you agree on the price. We will deliver as soon as we can, probably sometime next week.

Yours sincerely

Chris Masters
Management Trainee

Accepting an order (1)

1. The amended details should be repeated in this acceptance letter.

2. Once again, the letter is too brief, badly worded and vague.

3. A definite delivery date should be mentioned, along with the terms of payment.

Super Toys Ltd

Chattisfield Road, NEWTON NE12 0LD
Tel No: 2567 591048 Fax No: 2567 651987

25 February 199X

Mr Nigel Flack
The Animal Kingdom
Bruin Street
NEWTOWN
NE10 0PY

Dear Mr Flack

Further to our telephone conversation yesterday, we confirm that we are happy to accept your Order, number 346, subject to the alteration on the price of the Hedgehogs. These Hedgehogs will be charged as quoted at £1.50 each.

Your Order should be delivered on Wednesday 1 March at approximately 1500 hrs. As you have elected to pay cash on delivery, please ensure that you have the money ready to give to our driver. The total cost of the goods, including VAT, will be £1,598.

We thank you for your valued custom.

Yours sincerely

Sue Chapman (Miss)
Management Trainee

Accepting an Order (2)

1. Following telephone clarification, Sue has now made doubly sure that The Animal Kingdom know they are paying £1.50 for their Hedgehogs.

2. It is rather unusual to pay cash on delivery for such a large amount, but The Animal Kingdom are rather unusual, and possibly rather foolish, in as much as they like to deal in cash whenever possible.

3. Sue has, correctly, quoted a day and time for delivery.

POINTS FOR DISCUSSION

1. Why do you think it is very important for quotations and orders to be so explicit in their descriptions and prices of the goods in question?

2. How would you deal with a company who insisted they had been quoted £50.00 for a chair, when it should have been £500.00 and no trace of any paperwork could be found?

3. Why do you think it could be foolish for The Animal Kingdom to always pay their bills in cash?

7
Letters to Promote the Company

INTRODUCTION

In order to attract customers, a certain amount of promotion will need to take place. After all, if no-one knows about your company and what it does, not a lot of business will be generated.

Sales letters can play an important part in promotion. Well thought out letters sent to key companies and/or individuals can be very successful. By using a word processing program and the mail merge facility (see Chapter 5), this type of letter can not only look very professional and personalised, but also be very easy to prepare. A tear-off slip at the bottom to be returned by the recipient of the letter provides a definite lead for the sales force to follow up.

As far as media advertising is concerned, this will depend very much on the type of company. Large organisations may be able to advertise their wares on television, whilst smaller low budget companies will probably have to be content with an occasional 'ad' in the local paper.

Finally, it is very important for new and existing customers to be constantly reminded of the product/service you can offer to them. Regular mailings and, if appropriate, regular visits, can ensure that your company stays uppermost in your customers' minds.

For the sample letters in this Chapter we use Super Toys Ltd throughout.

The sample letters
The sample letters in this chapter illustrate the following:

Super Toys Ltd

Chattisfield Road, NEWTON NE12 0LD
Tel No: 2567 591048 Fax No: 2567 651987

21 March 199X

The Manager
The Toy Hamper
45 Church Street
NEWTOWN
NE4 9LP

Dear Sir

We are writing to ask if you would like to buy some of our new bears. They are really good and we have sold many.

Timothy Teddy Bear is 30 cm high and dark brown. He has an appealing face, and he talks, crawls and clings to people – with a little help from his batteries.

Why not try 20 or 30 teddies to start with? You can have some more later if you like them.

Give me a ring and we will sort something out.

Yours faithfully

Chris Masters
Management Trainee

Advertising company products/services (1)

1. Chris has not bothered to telephone the shop to check on the owner's name so that the letter can be personalised.

2. He has not given the price of the teddy bear.

3. The wording of the letter is a little disjointed in parts.

4. There is no 'carrot' to encourage people to buy.

Super Toys Ltd

Chattisfield Road, NEWTON NE12 0LD
Tel No: 2567 591048   Fax No: 2567 651987

21 March 199X

Miss Linda France
The Toy Hamper
45 Church Street
NEWTOWN
NE4 9LP

Dear Miss France

TIMOTHY TEDDY BEAR

We are writing to tell you about our brand-new product which, we think, will revolutionise the teddy bear world.

TIMOTHY TEDDY BEAR stands a full 30 cm high and is made of dark brown plush fur. He talks, crawls and even clings to people. He operates via 4 AA size rechargeable batteries.

TIMOTHY TEDDY BEAR will normally be £9.99 trade each, but for a limited period only we are offering you supplies at £7.50. Why not try 20 or even 30 at this very special price?

We know you will be pleased to hear that one of our representatives will call on you within the next few days to show you TIMOTHY TEDDY BEAR in person. We are sure that you will be as impressed as we are with this exciting new product.

Yours sincerely

Sue Chapman (Miss)
Management Trainee

Advertising company products/services (2)

This letter is informative, eye catching and gives emphasis to the product by showing TIMOTHY TEDDY BEAR in capitals.

Super Toys Ltd

Chattisfield Road, NEWTON NE12 0LD
Tel No: 2567 591048 Fax No: 2567 651987

1 April 199X

Dear Customer

We have an exciting new product just released onto the market. It is a teddy bear called Timothy Teddy Bear.

Timothy is a dark brown teddy, standing 30 cm high. He talks, crawls and clings to people. He sells at £9.99 trade normally, but we are offering him at £7.50 for now.

Order early by filling in the tear off slip below and returning it to us with your money, unless you have an account.

Yours sincerely

Chris Masters
Management Trainee

— —

Name...

Address ....

I would like ..... Timothy Teddy Bears @ £7.50 each

I enclose a cheque*
Please charge my account*   *Delete as applicable

Writing circular letters (1)

1. Chris has not given emphasis to the name of the teddy.

2. There are grammatical errors together with a distinct lack of information.

3. A full date is not normally inserted in a circular letter.

4. Not enough space has been left for the address on the tear off slip.

Super Toys Ltd

Chattisfield Road, NEWTON NE12 0LD
Tel No: 2567 591048   Fax No: 2567 651987

April 199X

Dear Customer

We are writing to tell you about our brand-new product which, we think, will revolutionise the teddy bear world.

TIMOTHY TEDDY BEAR stands a full 30 cm high and is made of dark brown plush fur. He talks, crawls and even clings to people. He operates via 4 AA size rechargeable batteries.

TIMOTHY TEDDY BEAR will normally be £9.99 trade each, but for a limited period only we are offering you supplies at £7.50.

To receive your TIMOTHY TEDDY BEARS, please fill in and return the tear-off slip below. Payment can be made with the order, or account customers can pay under the normal 30 day terms.

Yours sincerely

Sue Chapman (Miss)
Management Trainee

— —

Name..

Address ....

....

I would like ..... Timothy Teddy Bears @ £7.50 each

I enclose a cheque*
Please charge my account*   *Delete as applicable

Writing circular letters (2)

1. The letter and tear off slip are easy to understand and should prompt a positive reaction.

2. By showing just the month and year for the date the letters can be sent out throughout April.

Super Toys Ltd

Chattisfield Road, NEWTON NE12 0LD
Tel No: 2567 591048 Fax No: 2567 651987

20 April 199X

Classified Ads Manager
The Herald Weekly
65 Ship Street
NEWTOWN
NE2 8NH

Dear Sir

We want to place the enclosed advert in a local newspaper. We wonder what terms you would offer us?

If we get it cheaper for advertising for say a month rather than just for one week we might consider that.

Please let us know what you can do.

Yours faithfully

Chris Masters
Management Trainee

Enc

Approaching a newspaper about advertising (1)

1. Chris has omitted to find out the manager's name so that the letter can be personally addressed. This will not get him off to a good start.

2. No mention is made of the size of advertisement Super Toys are considering. In fact Chris gives very little detail at all.

3. A newspaper can become a 'good friend'. This letter is not likely to get Super Toys into the Editor's good books.

Super Toys Ltd

Chattisfield Road, NEWTON NE12 0LD
Tel No: 2567 591048 Fax No: 2567 651987

20 April 199X

Mr James Platt
Classified Advertisement Manager
The Herald Weekly
65 Ship Street
NEWTOWN
NE2 8NH

Dear Mr Platt

TIMOTHY TEDDY BEAR

As you will see from the enclosed advertisement, we are about to
launch the above product, and we would like to give it some good
publicity.

Having used your newspaper in the past with excellent results, we
are approaching you first this time to see what terms you can offer to
us. We would be prepared to go for a multiple insertion of say ten
issues if this would work out cheaper. The size of advertisement we
have in mind is approx ¼ page.

We look forward to hearing from you.

Yours sincerely

Sue Chapman
Management Trainee

Approaching a newspaper about advertising (2)

1. Sue has started out by addressing the manager in person and she has offered
   a little flattery in order to get a good deal.

2. The talk of a multiple insertion will interest Mr Platt. He should be keen to
   pursue the matter further.

Super Toys Ltd

Chattisfield Road, NEWTON NE12 0LD
Tel No: 2567 591048 Fax No: 2567 651987

22 April 199X

The Advertising Manager
Plus Time Television
NEWTOWN
NE1 9YH

Dear Sir

We would like to advertise on your television station. We are
particularly interested in daytime advertising as we want to advertise
bears. About 30 seconds should be enough about once a week.
How much would this cost? Please let us know your rates.

Yours faithfully

Chris Masters
Management Trainee

Approaching a TV company about advertising (1)

1. Well, this sort of letter is not going to 'wow' the Ad Manager. In fact, he or
   she is not likely to take it very seriously at all. Apart from the poor standard
   of grammar, there is not enough detail and 'bears' is too vague a description
   of what is to be advertised.

2. Once again, Chris has not bothered to find out the name of the manager.

Super Toys Ltd

Chattisfield Road, NEWTON NE12 0LD
Tel No: 2567 591048 Fax No: 2567 651987

22 April 199X

Ms Susy Hand
Advertising Manager
Plus Time Television
NEWTOWN
NE1 9YH

Dear Ms Hand

TIMOTHY TEDDY BEAR

We have a brand-new product available very soon, which we think
will revolutionise the teddy bear world.

TIMOTHY TEDDY BEAR is a dark brown, plush fur bear, which
talks, crawls and clings to people. He retails at £13.99 and we think
he will be a big seller.

In order to give our new bear maximum publicity we would like to
advertise on your television network. We are interested in a daytime
slot when plenty of children are viewing, and would like about 30
seconds once a week.

Please could you send us full details of your advertising rates and
perhaps suggest a day and time when our Director, Mr Paul Luck,
could call and see you to discuss this matter further.

Yours sincerely

Sue Chapman
Management Trainee

Approaching a TV company about advertising (2)

1. Sue has explained the situation clearly. Ms Hand now knows what Super
    Toys want to advertise, when and for how long.

2. The meeting with Sue's boss should finalise the arrangements.

Super Toys Ltd

Chattisfield Road, NEWTON NE12 0LD
Tel No: 2567 591048   Fax No: 2567 651987

Dear Colleagues

Sales Bulletin – Spring 199X

As some of you may know I'm going to be issuing a bulletin four
times a year from now on. It will help you all to see what is
happening to each other.

Sales Targets
These have only been met by 2 of you. This is disappointing. Only
Tim and Sue have met their targets. I shall expect better results in
the next quarter.

New Appointments
I am pleased to tell you that we have another sales person starting
next week. Her name is Mandy George and I hope you will all make
her welcome.

Holidays
Just to refresh your memories. You must give Julie your holiday
dates by 23 May. This will be for 1st June 19- - to 31 May 19 - -.
You are not allowed to take more than two weeks during the period
July – September inclusive.

That's it for now folks. Let me have any comments on my brief
offering.

Yours sincerely

Andrew Roach
Sales Manager

Giving encouragement to the sales force (1)

1. This is Andrew's first draft. He will need to give a date – just the month and
   year. The headings do not stand out enough, and the sentences are rather
   stilted. The 'Holidays' and 'New Appointments' paragraphs need to be
   reversed. Yours sincerely is an inappropriate ending.

2. Most importantly of all, this letter does not offer encouragement for the
   future.

Super Toys Ltd

Chattisfield Road, NEWTON NE12 0LD
Tel No: 2567 591048 Fax No: 2567 651987

May 199X

Dear Colleagues

Sales Bulletin – Spring 199X

As you may know, I am intending to issue a short bulletin four times a year so that we can all keep in touch with what is happening. This is the very first one, so here goes!

SALES TARGETS   I am sorry to say that only Tim and Sue have met their targets this quarter. I know times are hard, but I shall expect better results next time. Please do your very best. Bonuses will be high if your targets are met.

HOLIDAYS   Summer is just around the corner, so I would like to remind you all to let Julie have your holiday days by 23 May. The holiday year runs from 1 June 19- - to 31 May 19 - -. Please remember that you cannot take more than two weeks holiday leave during the period June to September inclusive.

NEW APPOINTMENTS   I am pleased to tell you that we have an additional sales person starting next week. Her name is Mandy George and I hope you will all make her welcome.

Even though targets have not been met, I would like to say that I have received nothing but praise from our customers, many of whom have written in to me personally, saying what a courteous and conscientious workforce we have. Please keep up the good work and don't forget that I am always here if you have any problems to discuss or comments to make on the future format of this bulletin.

Best wishes to you all.

Andrew Roach
Sales Manager

Giving encouragement to the sales force (2)

This letter speaks for itself. Although only brief, it is encouraging and motivating. It should keep everyone happy.

Super Toys Ltd

Chattisfield Road, NEWTON NE12 0LD
Tel No: 2567 591048 Fax No: 2567 651987

Our Ref AR/cm/7002

3 June 199X

Mr James Mooney
45 Townlands Walk
SHOTTERN
SH4 1YH

Dear Mr Mooney

You contacted us some time ago now about some soft toys. Unfortunately, you have not placed an order with us and we are wondering why.

Have you found someone else? If so, please let us know so that we do not send you any further information.

We look forward to hearing from you.

Yours sincerely

Chris Masters
Management Trainee

Following up new customers (1)

1. It is very important to follow up a potential new customer.

2. It is equally important for that follow up to be effective. This letter does make the relevant points, but not very tactfully, and it is not likely to send Mr Mooney rushing to the telephone to place an order with Super Toys!

Super Toys Ltd

Chattisfield Road, NEWTON NE12 0LD
Tel No: 2567 591048 Fax No: 2567 651987

Our Ref AR/cm/7002

3 June 199X

Mr James Mooney
45 Townlands Walk
SHOTTERN
SH4 1YH

Dear Mr Mooney

You may remember contacting our company some time ago, with regard to us supplying you with our high quality soft toys.

As we have not heard from you, we are wondering if we can offer you further information, or perhaps make an appointment to come and show you our full range of products.

If we can be of any further assistance to you, please do not hesitate to telephone us. We can then discuss your exact requirements in more detail.

Yours sincerely

Sue Chapman (Miss)
Management Trainee

Following up new customers (2)

This letter will serve as a gentle reminder to Mr Mooney of his contact with Super Toys. It could well prompt him into action, as he will, hopefully, feel encouraged by the time and effort taken to follow up his enquiry.

POINTS FOR DISCUSSION

1. Do you think of circular letters as 'junk mail'? If so, what can be done to make sure such letters are taken more seriously?

2. Compose a letter to the Editor of your local newspaper, Mr Peter Black of Holtring Evening News, 28 The Avenue, Newtown NE6 7JN. Ask him if he will print a free editorial telling local people about how your company are producing ten thousand teddy bears to send out to underprivileged children this Christmas.

3. How would you word a letter to one of your salespeople who was consistently failing to reach the targets expected by your company?

8
Letters Dealing with
Accounts Problems

INTRODUCTION

Even in our modern world of complex technology, accounting problems still occur. Although most accounts work is now computerised, errors do still creep in; this is mainly due to the human element in the form of the person who gives the computer the data to work from. After all, a machine is only as good as its operator. Very often writing down all the information in the form of a letter is the only way to sort out such problems.

Coping with bad payers
It is also a sad fact of life that many accounting problems involve people or companies who are either unable or unwilling to pay their bills. One company failing to pay a bill can have a 'knock on' effect, possibly causing hardship to many more companies who are themselves waiting for payment. This cash flow situation can get very serious, in some cases causing financial ruin to an innocent bystander who cannot continue trading due to bad debts. A well worded letter to a bad payer may achieve the desired result, and if nothing else will provide evidence to use in a court of law, as we have discussed before. Main problems:

- disputes over accounts issued by your company

- disputes over accounts issued to your company

- non payment of debts to your company

- changes to and queries on staff salaries

- miscellaneous one-off accounting errors.

The sample letters
The sample letters in this chapter illustrate the following:

The Animal Kingdom

Bruin Street, Newtown, NE10 0PY
Telephone: 3691 279017

Our Ref NF/CT/341

6 June 199X

Mr C Rogers
Accounts Manager
Super Toys Ltd
Chattisfield Road
NEWTOWN
NE12 0LD

Dear Mr Rogers

Re Your Account No. 7125 – dated 20 May 199X

We were very distressed to receive your account as above. As you know we always pay for our goods in cash and we therefore do not owe you anything. Please confirm that this is the case.

Yours sincerely

Nigel Flack
Partner

Disputing an account (1)

1. This letter is rather blunt, presumably because Nigel is rather annoyed.

2. It would help Super Toys, however, if Nigel stated when the case payment was made and for how much, so that Super Toys can check back in their records.

The Animal Kingdom

Bruin Street, Newtown, NE10 0PY
Telephone: 3691 279017

Our Ref JB/CT/341

6 June 199X

Mr C Rogers
Accounts Manager
Super Toys Ltd
Chattisfield Road
NEWTOWN
NE12 0LD

Dear Mr Rogers

Re Your Account No. 7125 – dated 20 May 199X

We were a little disturbed to receive the above account for goods delivered to us in April.

As we are sure you are aware, we always pay for our goods in cash, and on 24 April when the goods in question were delivered, we gave the driver £534.00 in full payment. A photocopy of the receipt given to us by your driver, Jack Briggs, is enclosed.

Would you please be kind enough to check your records and then confirm to us that our account is clear.

Yours sincerely

Jenny Bateman (Miss)
Partner
Enc

Disputing an account (2)

1. Jenny, like Nigel, is justifiably annoyed, but she has taken the time and trouble to explain the situation fully. Sending the photocopy of the receipt is a good idea, too.

2. Hopefully when Super Toys have checked their records this matter will be resolved.

Softy Fabrics

3 Denmark Rise · Newtown · NE3 1YH
Tel: 3468 714856 · Fax: 3468 718921

Your Ref
Our Ref BF/SS/6301

10 June 199X

Brook & Son Toymakers
61-71 Steel Street
BRIDGETOWN
BR61 7RE

Dear Sirs

We supplied you with a considerable amount of fur
material on 1 April and we have not received
payment of the amount due.

This account is now considerably overdue and we
would appreciate your cheque in full settlement by
return.

Yours sincerely

Sara Smythe (Ms)
Management Trainee

Chasing a debt (1)

1. You might think this letter is brief, to the point and adequate. It does not, however, state the amount due or the account number for Brook & Son to refer back to.

2. It is usual in a letter such as this to add that if payment has already been sent the letter can be disregarded.

3. A letter beginning with Dear Sirs, should end with Yours faithfully.

Softy Fabrics

3 Denmark Rise · Newtown · NE3 1YH
Tel: 3468 714856 · Fax: 3468 718921

Your Ref
Our Ref BF/SP/6301

10 June 199X

Brook & Son Toymakers
61-71 Steel Street
BRIDGETOWN
BR61 7RE

Dear Sirs

Account No 6301, £650.00, dated 21 April 19--

The above account, in respect of the fur material
supplied to you on 1 April, is now considerably
overdue.

May we remind you that our terms of trade are
strictly 30 days, and we would therefore
appreciate your payment by return.

If you have already made payment to us by the
time you receive this letter, then please accept
our thanks for settling the account.

Yours faithfully

Simon Palmer
Management Trainee

Chasing a debt (2)

1. Brian Fuller, who has asked the trainees to prepare this letter, is likely to be far happier with this version than with Sara's.

2. Simon's letter is formal, but not too much so. It gives the account number and full details. It states the case with no frills, and politely recognises that a cheque in settlement may have crossed in the post.

Softy Fabrics

3 Denmark Rise · Newtown · NE3 1YH
Tel: 3468 714856 · Fax: 3468 718921

Your Ref
Our Ref BF/SS/6301

10 August 199X

Brook & Son Toymakers
61-71 Steel Street
BRIDGETOWN
BR61 7RE

Dear Sirs

We still have not received a cheque from you for
the amount due on our Account No 6301.

We therefore have no alternative but to take legal
action to recover the debt and you will be hearing
from our solicitors very soon.

We will not deal with your company ever again
after this experience.

Yours faithfully

Sara Smythe (Ms)
Management Trainee

Sending a final demand (1)

1. This letter does not give all the necessary information: the outstanding
    amount has not been mentioned, nor have the dates of any previous
    reminders.

2. Although it might be stating the truth, the last paragraph is unnecessary at
    this stage. It sounds rather like playground talk. You would hear a young
    child shout to a friend, 'I'm not going to play with you ever again', when
    something goes wrong! Future business can be discussed at a later date.

Softy Fabrics

3 Denmark Rise · Newtown · NE3 1YH
Tel: 3468 714856 · Fax: 3468 718921

```
Your Ref
Our Ref BF/SP/6301

10 August 199X

Brook & Son Toymakers
61-71 Steel Street
BRIDGETOWN
BR61 7RE

Dear Sirs

Account No 3601
1st Reminder sent - 10 June 199X
2nd Reminder sent - 10 July 199X

Despite repeated reminders by letter and telephone,
we have still not received your cheque to clear
the above overdue account.

Unless we hear from you by return, we shall have
no alternative but to take legal action to recover
the debt, and you will be hearing from our
solicitors shortly.

Yours faithfully



Simon Palmer
Management Trainee
```

Sending a final demand (2)

All the relevant details are given here. Brook & Son can be in no doubt as to what is going to happen next if they choose not to pay up.

Super Toys Ltd

Chattisfield Road, NEWTON NE12 0LD
Fax No: 2567 591048 Fax No: 2567 651987

28 August 199X

Mr Nigel Flack
The Animal Kingdom
Bruin Street
NEWTOWN
NE10 0PY

Dear Mr Flack

Sorry to have to write to you about the accounts below, but we seem to be in a bit of a muddle over them. Could you have a look and let us know accordingly.

Account No 304681 dated 20 June 199X £185.00 – paid in cash

Account No 314523 dated 10 July 199X £356.00 – not paid

Account No 316431 dated 28 July 199X £256.00 – not paid

Account No 321523 dated 10 Aug 199X £320.00 – paid in cash

It seems strange that our records say you have not paid two of these accounts.

Yours sincerely

Chris Masters
Management Trainee

Sorting out an accounts muddle (1)

1. This letter is disjointed and although the facts are there they are badly presented.

2. Although Super Toys may be in a muddle, it would be better not to admit this in black and white!

Super Toys Ltd

Chattisfield Road, NEWTON NE12 0LD
Fax No: 2567 591048 Fax No: 2567 651987

28 August 199X

Mr Nigel Flack
The Animal Kingdom
Bruin Street
NEWTOWN
NE10 0PY

Dear Mr Flack

Our records show a discrepancy in payment of two of the following accounts.

Account No 304681 dated 20 June 199X £185.00 – paid in cash

Account No 314523 dated 10 July 199X £356.00 – not paid

Account No 316431 dated 28 July 199X £256.00 – not paid

Account No 321523 dated 10 Aug 199X £320.00 – paid in cash

As you will see, according to our records, Account No 314523 and Account No 316431 have not been paid.

Would you please be kind enough to check back in your Accounts for these two payments and confirm your findings to us as soon as possible.

Yours sincerely

Sue Chapman (Miss)
Management Trainee

Sorting out an accounts muddle (2)

This letter is clearer and even though the subject matter is none too pleasant, Sue has been polite. At this stage she is not actually accusing The Animal Kingdom of non payment; she is leaving the way open for a logical explanation.

Super Toys Ltd

Chattisfield Road, NEWTON NE12 0LD
Fax No: 2567 591048 Fax No: 2567 651987

5 September 199X

Mr Nigel Flack
The Animal Kingdom
Bruin Street
NEWTOWN
NE10 0PY

Dear Mr Flack

Account No 314523 dated 10 July 199X £356.00
Account No 316431 dated 28 July 199X £256.00

Sorry about the mix up over these. As we discussed the problem was that two of your cash payments had been entered into the wrong account. Perhaps you should use cheques after all!

We value your custom so we hope you will accept our apology and continue trading with us.

Yours sincerely

Chris Masters
Management Trainee

Apologising for an accounting error (1)

Would this letter make *you* want to carry on trading with Super Toys? Probably not! The letter is very offhand, treating what is quite a serious matter in a lighthearted fashion. Even the apology does not sound genuine.

Super Toys Ltd

Chattisfield Road, NEWTON NE12 0LD
Fax No: 2567 591048 Fax No: 2567 651987

5 September 199X

Mr Nigel Flack
The Animal Kingdom
Bruin Street
NEWTOWN
NE10 0PY

Dear Mr Flack

Account No 314523 dated 10 July 199X   £356.00
Account No 316431 dated 28 July 199X   £256.00

Thank you for your telephone call with regard to this matter and for
the information that you gave to us.

We can only apologise for what is entirely our error. The cash you
paid in settlement of these two accounts was unfortunately paid into
the wrong account. There is absolutely no excuse for this at all, and
all we can do is say we are very sorry that the mix-up occurred.

We do value your custom and would not want this incident to spoil
the special business relationship we have enjoyed in the past. You
will, we are sure, appreciate that we do have to investigate
accounting discrepancies, but we sincerely hope that a situation
such as this will not arise again in the future.

Yours sincerely

Sue Chapman (Miss)
Management Trainee

Apologising for an accounting error (2)

1. This letter is far more likely to achieve the desired effect. Sue has repeatedly
    apologised and has admitted, correctly, that Super Toys are wholly
    responsible for the error.

2. Honesty is always the best policy and The Animal Kingdom should
    appreciate this approach.

Super Toys Ltd

Chattisfield Road, NEWTON NE12 0LD
Fax No: 2567 591048 Fax No: 2567 651987

August 199X

Dear Colleagues

I am writing to advise you of an increase in your salary, to take place as from 1 October 199X. The company is planning to increase your salary by 2 per cent per annum.

Although this increase is not great, it is all the company can afford in these difficult trading times. I hope you will understand this and that you will work with us to make the company as profitable as possible in the future.

Yours sincerely

Angie Young (Mrs)
Personnel Manager

Advising staff about salary change (1)

1. This is Angie's first draft copy. The wording can be improved as shown in version 2.

2. When writing a letter such as this it is important to get the staff on your side; make them feel that the company is being as generous as possible. The last thing anyone wants is a strike or mass resignations to cope with. If the staff know the company is doing its best they are far more likely to remain loyal than if they think they are being 'conned'.

Super Toys Ltd

Chattisfield Road, NEWTON NE12 0LD
Fax No: 2567 591048 Fax No: 2567 651987

August 199X

Dear Colleagues

As from 1 October 199X the company is planning to increase your salary by two per cent per annum.

This increase is not as high as we would have hoped, but unfortunately it is all we can afford in these difficult trading times. We are trying to avoid any redundancies and a modest pay rise is the only option open to us.

We hope you will understand the current situation and that you will work with us to make the company as profitable as possible in the months to come.

Yours sincerely

Angie Young (Mrs)
Personnel Manager

Advising staff about salary change (2)

1. This is an amended version of the previous letter.

2. The staff should feel some sympathy with the company's situation from the wording of this second attempt. They may feel peeved about the small increase, but they will probably also feel grateful that they still have a job.

POINTS FOR DISCUSSION

1. How do you think people could cut down on the number of accounting errors made in business today?

2. Compose a letter to someone you have thought of as a friend. This friend has fallen on hard times and cannot afford to pay your bill for secretarial services. The amount is £200.00 and you have been waiting for three months. What would you say to them?

3. Write to The Animal Kingdom tactfully suggesting that they should pay all their future bills by cheque or Bank Giro Credit rather than by cash. Sign the letter as Sue Chapman of Super Toys Ltd.

How to Write a Report

John Bowden
Second edition

Written by an experienced manager and staff trainer, this well-presented handbook provides a very clear step-by-step framework for every individual, whether dealing with professional advisers, banks, customers, clients, suppliers or junior or senior staff. Contents: Preparation and planning. Collecting and handling information. Writing a report. Improving your thinking. Improving presentation. Achieving a good writing style. Making effective use of English. Illustrations. Choosing paper, covers and binding. Appendices, glossary, index. John Bowden BSc(Econ) MSc has long experience both as a professional manager in industry, and as a Senior Lecturer running numerous courses in accountancy, auditing, and effective communication, up to senior management level.

£7.99, 160pp illus. 1 85703 091 5. Please add postage & packing (UK £1 per copy, Europe £2 per copy, World £3 per copy airmail).

How To Books Ltd, Plymbridge House, Estover Road, Plymouth PL6 7PZ. United Kingdom. Tel: (01752) 695745. Fax: (01752) 695699. Tele: 45635.

Credit card orders may be faxed or phoned.

9
Letters on Staff Matters

Without employees an organisation cannot function and, generally speaking, the more efficient and content the workforce, the more successful the organisation. It should be remembered, therefore, that dealings with staff are just as important as those with other people.

Sometimes unpleasant tasks such as writing a warning letter, or even a dismissal letter, have to be undertaken. This kind of letter is not easy to compose. A certain amount of tact and sympathy is necessary. After all, the person you are writing to has real feelings, just like you.

Sorting out staff problems is another area where tact and understanding will help you to get to the root of the trouble. Personality clashes, for instance, are commonplace and must be contained.

Most correspondence in connection with staff is pleasant, rather than unpleasant, in nature. Letters of appointment, references and appraisals, form the positive, routine work of a typical employer.

All correspondence concerning staff – whatever its purpose – should be treated as strictly confidential. You should never discuss a staff letter with anyone who does not already know its contents. So called scandal can spread very rapidly, often becoming totally distorted along the way.

The sample letters
Angie Young, the Personnel Manager at Softy Toys, wants to give Sue Chapman some experience. Sue prepares each letter first. Angie reads it and then shows her own version for comparison purposes. All letters are to be signed by Angie.

Super Toys Ltd

Chattisfield Road, NEWTON NE12 0LD
Tel No: 2567 591048 Fax No: 2567 651987

10 September 199X

CONFIDENTIAL

Miss V Sharpe
65 Ocean Square
NEWTOWN
NE21 0BE

Dear Miss Sharpe

Thank you for attending for an interview last Tuesday.

As you know, we had a huge response to our advertisement and we are sorry to say that on this occasion you were not successful. The standard of applicants was high and we found it hard to reach a decision.

Good luck with future applications.

Yours sincerely

Angie Young (Ms)
PERSONNEL MANAGER

Contacting an unsuccessful job applicant (1)

1. The job applied for should be stated in a heading at the beginning of the letter.
2. Sue does not give the job applicant much reason to feel confident about her future. Miss Sharpe has done well to reach the interview stage and more should be made of her efforts. Suggesting she apply for any future vacancies with the company would be a way of making her feel worthwhile rather than dismissed for ever.
3. The last paragraph is uncaringly brief.

Super Toys Ltd

Chattisfield Road, NEWTON NE12 0LD
Tel No: 2567 591048 Fax No: 2567 651987

10 September 199X

CONFIDENTIAL

Miss V Sharpe
65 Ocean Square
NEWTOWN
NE21 0BE

Dear Miss Sharpe

APPOINTMENT OF JUNIOR PERSONNEL OFFICER

Thank you very much for attending an interview last week.

We had an unprecedented response to our advertisement, reflecting, no doubt, the effects of the present recession. This meant we found it very hard to choose just one person from the many applicants, yourself included, who had the experience, qualifications and personality we were looking for.

We do wish you every success in finding a suitable position. If we advertise a vacancy here in the future, please feel free to apply, and we will consider your application very seriously.

Yours sincerely

Angie Young (Ms)
PERSONNEL MANAGER

Contacting an unsuccessful job applicant (2)

1. This friendly letter should make Miss Sharpe feel she was a close second – even if she wasn't! There is nothing wrong with a bit of ego boosting, especially with the fierce competition for jobs that exists at the present time. It should give her hope for the future, and leave her with a good impression of Super Toys.
2. Many people consider this type of letter very hard to write, but as long as you can find some way of showing the person that they were just unlucky rather than unsuitable, they will have the confidence to continue their job search.

Super Toys Ltd

Chattisfield Road, NEWTON NE12 0LD
Tel No: 2567 591048 Fax No: 2567 651987

10 September 199X

CONFIDENTIAL

Mrs P Snowe
The Ridings
NEWTOWN
NE14 6TY

Dear Mrs Snowe

APPOINTMENT OF JUNIOR PERSONNEL OFFICER

Further to our telephone conversation yesterday, I am delighted to confirm your appointment as Junior Personnel Officer.

I am enclosing two copies of our Contract. Please sign and return one to us. A medical will be arranged for later this week, and we will telephone you with the details.

We look forward to you joining us next month.

Yours sincerely

Angie Young (Ms)
PERSONNEL MANAGER

enc

Sending a letter of appointment (1)

The contents of this letter are fine – as far as they go. Although a contract is being enclosed, mention should still be made of the most important points of the job appointment, such as date of commencement, salary, working hours, holidays, and probationary period.

Super Toys Ltd

Chattisfield Road, NEWTON NE12 0LD
Tel No: 2567 591048 Fax No: 2567 651987

10 September 199X

CONFIDENTIAL

Mrs P Snowe
The Ridings
NEWTOWN
NE14 6TY

Dear Mrs Snowe

APPOINTMENT OF JUNIOR PERSONNEL OFFICER

Further to our telephone conversation yesterday, I am delighted to confirm
your appointment as Junior Personnel Officer, commencing on 1 October
199X.

You will find enclosed two copies of our Contract of Employment. Please
sign and return one copy to us as soon as possible. Once I have received
your signed Contract, an appointment will be made for you to have a
medical, and I will telephone you to arrange a day for this.

Your hours of work will be from 0900 hrs to 1700 hrs, Monday to Friday
with one hour for lunch. Holiday entitlement is 4 weeks each year. You will
serve a probationary period of three months, during which time your salary
will be £9,000 per annum. After satisfactory completion of the probationary
period your salary will rise to £10,000 per annum. One month's notice is
required if you wish to leave the company.

I look forward to welcoming you to Super Toys and hope that you will be
very happy with us.

Yours sincerely

Angie Young (Ms)
PERSONNEL MANAGER

Enc

Sending a letter of appointment (2)

This is a friendly, positive letter, setting out all the relevant points for Mrs Snowe
to digest.

Super Toys Ltd

Chattisfield Road, NEWTON NE12 0LD
Tel No: 2567 591048 Fax No: 2567 651987

Your Ref RHD/CWT

10 September 199X

CONFIDENTIAL

Mr R H Dean
Dean & Co
Pride View
NEWTOWN
NE34 8WS

Dear Mr Dean

<u>James C Scott</u>

Mr Scott was employed by Super Toys Ltd from June 1988 to August 1992. He was employed as a Sales Representative. He was conscientious and reliable.

He should make a good member of your staff.

Yours sincerely

Angie Young (Ms)
PERSONNEL MANAGER

Giving a favourable reference (1)

1. No mention is made of a letter or telephone call from Mr Dean asking for this reference.
2. Mr Dean will probably wish he hadn't bothered to ask anyway if he receives this. Admittedly it does tell him that James Scott was employed by Super Toys and that he was conscientious and reliable, but a little more detail is necessary. For instance. how did Mr Scott mix with other members of staff?
3. In addition, some enthusiasm needs to be shown so that Mr Dean feels convinced that James really would make a good employee.

Super Toys Ltd

Chattisfield Road, NEWTON NE12 0LD
Tel No: 2567 591048 Fax No: 2567 651987

Your Ref: RHD/CWT

10 September 199X

CONFIDENTIAL

Mr R H Dean
Dean & Co
Pride View
NEWTOWN
NE34 8WS

Dear Mr Dean

James C Scott

Thank you for your letter of 20 September requesting a reference on James C Scott.

Mr Scott was employed here as a sales representative, between June 1988 and August 1992. During his time with us he proved himself to be a reliable, conscientious and hard working man. He got on well with both his working colleagues and our customers. In fact, many customers expressed their regret when they heard that he was leaving.

I have no hesitation whatsoever in recommending Mr Scott for a position with your Company. I am sure he will prove to be a loyal and valued member of your team.

Yours sincerely

Angie Young (Ms)
PERSONNEL MANAGER

Giving a favourable reference (2)

This letter sounds much more enthusiastic about Mr Scott's talents. The information given is positive and informative, Mr Dean will know that if he decides to appoint Mr Scott, he can expect a good hard working employee who gets on well with other people.

Super Toys Ltd

Chattisfield Road, NEWTON NE12 0LD
Tel No: 2567 591048 Fax No: 2567 651987

1 October 199X

CONFIDENTIAL

Mrs June Rose
1 The Croft
NEWTOWN
NE10 PJY

Dear Mrs Rose

First written warning

You have already received two verbal warnings from me on
10 August and 10 September with regard to your unreasonable
behaviour at work. Unfortunately no improvement has been shown
to date.

Further to our informal meeting today I now intend to give you 14
days in which to improve both your attitude and your timekeeping.

I hope you will see that this matter is very serious and respond
appropriately.

Yours sincerely

Angie Young (Ms)
PERSONNEL MANAGER

Issuing a first warning (1)

Although Sue has composed this letter very well, she has omitted to give details
of what Mrs Rose's unreasonable behaviour actually is. It is very important that
every complaint is listed in detail, just in case Mrs Rose is dismissed and decides
to make a claim for Unfair Dismissal at an Industrial Tribunal.

Super Toys Ltd

Chattisfield Road, NEWTON NE12 0LD
Tel No: 2567 591048 Fax No: 2567 651987

1 October 199X

CONFIDENTIAL

Mrs June Rose
1 The Croft
NEWTOWN
NE10 PJY

Dear Mrs Rose

First written warning

You have already received two verbal warnings from me on 10 August and 10 September with regard to your unreasonable behaviour at work. Unfortunately no improvement has been shown to date.

Specifically this unreasonable behaviour involves:

1   Rudeness to Mrs Platt, your Supervisor
2   Lack of co-operation when asked to complete your work by a certain time
3   Failure to carry out all tasks listed on your Job Description
4   Persistent poor timekeeping

Further to our meeting today I intend to give you 14 days in which to improve your attitude to work and your timekeeping.

I hope you will see that this matter is very serious and respond appropriately.

Yours sincerely

Angie Young (Ms)
PERSONNEL MANAGER

Issuing a first warning (2)

Mrs Rose now has the situation fully explained to her in writing. Super Toys have written evidence should they need it.

Super Toys Ltd

Chattisfield Road, NEWTON NE12 0LD
Tel No: 2567 591048 Fax No: 2567 651987

16 October 199X

CONFIDENTIAL

Mrs June Rose
1 The Croft
NEWTOWN
NE10 PJY

Dear Mrs Rose

Second written warning

You will remember that we met on 1 October to discuss your general behaviour at work and your poor timekeeping. This meeting was followed up by a formal written warning letter sent to you on the same day.

Your behaviour has not improved and unless it does so within the next 7 days we shall be forced to dismiss you from the company.

Yours sincerely

Angie Young (Ms)
PERSONNEL MANAGER

Issuing a second warning (1)

Sue has once again made the letter sound rather vague. Specific grievances are not mentioned and this letter would serve very little purpose at an Industrial Tribunal.

Super Toys Ltd

Chattisfield Road, NEWTON NE12 0LD
Tel No: 2567 591048 Fax No: 2567 651987

16 October 199X

CONFIDENTIAL

Mrs June Rose
1 The Croft
NEWTOWN
NE10 PJY

Dear Mrs Rose

Second written warning

You will remember that we met on 1 October to discuss your general behaviour at work and your poor timekeeping. This meeting was followed by a formal written warning letter sent to you on the same day. This letter stated your unreasonable behaviour to include:

1   Rudeness to Mrs Platt, your Supervisor
2   Lack of co-operation when asked to complete your work by a certain time
3   Failure to carry out all tasks listed on your Job Description
4   Persistent poor timekeeping

We do try at Super Toys to give all our employees every possible chance to put right any unacceptable behaviour. You have now received 2 verbal and 2 written warnings, so far with no effect. Unless we see a definite improvement within 7 days, we shall be forced to dismiss you from the company.

Yours sincerely

Angie Young (Ms)
PERSONNEL MANAGER

Issuing a second warning (2)

Angie has listed the grievances again firstly for Mrs Rose and secondly to provide evidence for a Tribunal if necessary.

Super Toys Ltd

Chattisfield Road, NEWTON NE12 0LD
Tel No: 2567 591048 Fax No: 2567 651987

24 October 199X

CONFIDENTIAL

Mrs June Rose
1 The Croft
NEWTOWN
NE10 PJY

Dear Mrs Rose

This is to confirm that as from 31 October 199X you will no longer
be employed by this company. This follows 2 verbal warnings and 2
written warnings.

We are sorry that no other course of action is available to us and we
hope that you will be able to find alternative employment in the
future.

Yours sincerely

Angie Young (Ms)
PERSONNEL MANAGER

Writing a letter of dismissal (1)

1. The dates of the verbal and written warnings should be given for the record.
   These are included in version 2.
2. In this case, Mrs Rose was only employed on a weekly basis so she is only
   being given one week's notice. This notice will vary according to the
   employee's contract of employment.
3. Dismissal 'on the spot' (**summary dismissal**) is still a lawful possibility for
   very serious offences such as theft, or sexual harassment, but substantial
   evidence to support such allegations would have to be obtained first.

Super Toys Ltd

Chattisfield Road, NEWTON NE12 0LD
Tel No: 2567 591048 Fax No: 2567 651987

24 October 199X

CONFIDENTIAL

Mrs June Rose
1 The Croft
NEWTOWN
NE10 PJY

Dear Mrs Rose

This is to confirm that as from 31 October 199X you will no longer
be employed by this company. This follows verbal warnings on
19 August and 10 September and written warnings on 1 October
and 16 October.

We are sorry that no other course of action is available to us and we
hope that you will be able to find alternative employment in the
future.

Yours sincerely

Angie Young (Ms)
PERSONNEL MANAGER

Writing a letter of dismissal (2)

1. This letter, unwelcome though it may be, states the case as it stands and tells
   Mrs Rose that she has quite definitely been dismissed from the company.

2. Copies of all such correspondence should be kept for some considerable
   time, just in case the employee decides to fight the grounds for dismissal.

Super Toys Ltd

Chattisfield Road, NEWTON NE12 0LD
Tel No: 2567 591048 Fax No: 2567 651987

26 October 199X

CONFIDENTIAL

Miss Sue Chapman
65 The Common
NEWTOWN
NE8 9LD

Dear Sue

This letter is just to put into writing what we decided at our informal discussion last week, when we talked about you being unhappy working in the Sales Department.

Although it is obviously necessary for you to gain experience in all departments, you have now completed your 3 months in Sales, so it is time for you to move on anyway.

As from next week you will be working with me in the Personnel Department for 2 months. I understand you are interested in personnel work so perhaps this will make you happier.

I am glad you came to see me and I hope that when your training is finished we will be able to settle you into the department of your choice.

Yours sincerely

Angie Young (Ms)
PERSONNEL MANAGER

Sorting out a staff problem (1)

1. Sue spoke to Angie because she was very unhappy working in the Sales Department. She was on the point of leaving rather than continue in Sales, but Angie persuaded her to stay. Sue's shyness was a problem when it came to selling, and she used to worry a lot about having to persuade people to buy products they might not really want.

2. The wording of this letter is improved in the second version.

Super Toys Ltd

Chattisfield Road, NEWTON NE12 0LD
Tel No: 2567 591048 Fax No: 2567 651987

24 October 199X

CONFIDENTIAL

Miss Sue Chapman
65 The Common
NEWTOWN
NE8 9LD

Dear Sue

I am sending this letter to you in confirmation of our informal
discussion last week.

At that discussion you told me that you were unhappy working in the
Sales Department. As I explained, you must gain experience in all
departments of the company, including sales, if you are to be offered
a management position at the end of your training.

As you have nearly completed your 3 months in Sales, however, we
have decided to move you on to your next department. As from next
week, therefore, you will be working with me in the Personnel
Department. You told me that you were particularly interested in
personnel work so this move should make you feel happier and
more at ease.

I am glad you came to see me and I hope that when your training is
finished we will be able to settle you into the department of your
choice.

Yours sincerely

Angie Young (Ms)
PERSONNEL MANAGER

Sorting out a staff problem (2)

Angie has managed a more friendly approach here. Sue should feel reassured and
encouraged to carry on at Super Toys.

POINTS FOR DISCUSSION

1. Prepare a letter to send to a job applicant, Stephen Brown, telling him that he has not been successful in his bid to become a sales representative. Stephen already works for your company in the sales office and he felt sure that he would be offered the job. Say that he should apply again when another vacancy arises and that you are sorry about the outcome.

2. 'When an employer is asked for a reference he or she nearly always gives a good one'. Do you agree with this statement? If so, do you think employers should be more honest?

3. What would you do if you received what you felt to be an unjustified written warning? Would you write a letter back, or would you speak to the person concerned face to face?

10
Letters for Overseas

INTRODUCTION

Dealing with overseas companies and organisations is commonplace in business today. For this reason many UK companies will ask for potential employees to speak and write a second, or even third, language when they advertise job vacancies.

Not all of us can speak or write a foreign language fluently, however, but as English is the international language fortunately most people abroad will understand a letter written in English. It is certainly far better to write a good letter in English than a disastrously bad letter in another language, although the recipient might appreciate your efforts to try to please them.

Buying and selling, or importing and exporting, as it is called, forms the basis for the vast majority of business correspondence between ourselves and our overseas colleagues.

It is just as vital to form good business relationships abroad as it is in this country, and letters usually mark the start of that relationship. The same high standards of letter writing need to be applied, with the added proviso that it is even more important to keep the language clear, plain and easy to understand.

GENERAL POINTS TO REMEMBER

- Keep the words very simple and do not use very colloquial English expressions such as 'under the weather', 'a different ball game', 'sorting out the men from the boys'. A foreign reader would find these hard to understand.

- Only write in the language of the country if you are capable of doing so successfully. Otherwise good plain English will suffice.

- Make sure you give the person their correct title, for example Monsieur or M (French), or Herr (German).

- Always state on the envelope a postcode or 'zip code' and the country of destination when sending a letter overseas. It is best to put the country in capitals.

- Check that you have correctly interpreted the address. Sometimes telephone numbers can follow straight on from the address and this can cause confusion.

- Be prepared for a time delay. Do not expect a reply to your letter immediately.

- Because of the time delay, if the matter is urgent a telephone call might be a better alternative. If a letter is definitely necessary, it might be better to send it by fax (see Chapter 1).

IMPORTING AND EXPORTING GOODS

Goods are imported from overseas to sell in this country. These goods have to be shipped, or sent by air, and distributed once they arrive. In the same way, we export goods from our country to overseas markets, often using an agent or distributor to market the goods abroad.

The main complications with importing and exporting goods arise from the various commercial procedures that need to be carried out. These include arranging the method of payment to be used for buying the goods, and the means of transport.

The actual routine correspondence with a company or organisation overseas is much the same as takes place when buying and selling goods in this country, although some of the terminology is different.

In the examples which follow mention is made of a **bill of exchange**. This is an order in writing addressed by one person to another, signed by the person giving it, requiring the person to whom it is addressed to pay on demand a certain sum of money. In other words, it is just one of the many methods of transferring money abroad.

The sample letters

The sample letters in this chapter illustrate the following:

ADDRESSING OVERSEAS ENVELOPES

Example of an envelope addressed to the British Embassy in Italy:

British Embassy
Via XX Settembre 80A
00187 Rome
ITALY

Example of an envelope addressed to the British Embassy in South Africa:

British Embassy
91 Parliament Street
Cape Town 8001
SOUTH AFRICA

Ways of sending letters abroad

- By Airmail. Remember to either attach an Airmail sticker or write 'Par Avion – By Airmail' in the top left hand corner of your envelope. Delivery usually takes 3-4 days in Europe and 4-7 days outside Europe.
- By pre-paid Airmail products such as Swiftpacks and Aerogrammes. Your Post Office will give you details.
- By Surface Mail. Cheaper than Airmail but delivery takes longer – up to 2 weeks for Europe and 12 weeks outside Europe.

Super Toys Ltd

Chattisfield Road, NEWTON NE12 0LD
Tel No: 2567 591048 Fax No: 2567 651987

15 July 199X

Senora P Ferraro
Prole SA
S-1234 Madrid
SPAIN

Dear Senora Ferraro

TIMOTHY TEDDY BEAR

Thank you for your interest in our new product. We expect we will be able to let you have some bears if you can tell us how many you want.

We will require at least 50% payment in advance and the rest within 30 days of delivery. Will this be okay with you?

We look forward to hearing from you.

Yours sincerely

Chris Masters
Management Trainee

Seeking new business abroad (1)

1. Andrew Roach, the Sales Manager has asked Chris to try writing this letter, but he is not very pleased with the result.
2. The letter is not particularly friendly and would not make Senora Ferraro think that Super Toys are keen to export to them. Slang such as 'okay' should not be used in any business letters, especially for overseas.
3. No mention has been made of sending Senora Ferraro some samples to look at, as is usual practice.
4. Andrew decides to write the letter himself as shown in version 2.

Super Toys Ltd

Chattisfield Road, NEWTON NE12 0LD
Tel No: 2567 591048 Fax No: 2567 651987

15 July 199X

Senora P Ferraro
Prole SA
S-1234 Madrid
SPAIN

Dear Senora Ferraro

TIMOTHY TEDDY BEAR

Thank you for your interest in our exciting new product. We are sure that TIMOTHY TEDDY BEAR will prove to be a huge success in Spain.

Perhaps you could let us have some idea of the stocks you would be able to hold at any one time and what quantity you expect to be able to sell in the first year.

Please note that we require 50% payment in advance, for your first order, the remaining 50% payable 30 days after delivery. Future orders are subject to our normal credit terms.

We are sending you samples of TIMOTHY TEDDY BEAR, so that you can investigate the market further.

Yours sincerely

Andrew Roach
Sales Manager

Seeking new business abroad (2)

1. This is an informative, as well as enquiring, sales letter.

2. If he did not receive a reply, Andrew would follow it up a few weeks later to check on Senora Ferraro's position.

Super Toys Ltd

Chattisfield Road, NEWTON NE12 0LD
Tel No: 2567 591048 Fax No: 2567 651987

Our Ref: Agency 231

11 August 199X

Monsieur Pierre Levaux
342 rue de la Bain
234 Paris
FRANCE

Dear Monsieur Levaux

Agency with Super Toys Limited

This letter is to offer you the position of agent to cover our interests in France.

The Agency would begin on 1 September 19- - and run initially for two years. You would take our goods on a consignment basis and we would offer a discount of 30 per cent off the list price for all stock sold. You would need to store our stock properly. The stock would be brought to you by road, via the Channel Tunnel.

We would also provide samples, free of charge, for you to show your clients.

Please confirm your acceptance, in principle, of this offer. When we receive this we will forward to you an official Agreement for you to sign.

Yours sincerely

Andrew Roach
Sales Manager

Appointing an overseas agent (1)

1. Andrew has asked Chris to prepare this letter for him. It contains the relevant points but they are not displayed to good effect.

2. In the next example Andrew has improved on the presentation.

Super Toys Ltd

Chattisfield Road, NEWTON NE12 0LD
Tel No: 2567 591048 Fax No: 2567 651987

Our Ref: Agency 231

11 August 199X

Monsieur Pierre Levaux
342 rue de la Bain
234 Paris
FRANCE

Dear Monsieur Levaux

Agency with Super Toys Limited

We are pleased to offer you the position of Agent to cover our interests in France. The terms of the Agency would be as follows:

1   The Agency to commence on 1 September 199X and run initially for two years.
2   Goods to be taken on a consignment basis with a discount of 30 per cent off the list price for all stock sold.
3   All stock to be stored correctly.
4   Stock to be brought by road via the Channel Tunnel.
5   Samples to be provided to you free of charge, by ourselves, for you to show to your clients.

If these terms are acceptable to you in principle, please confirm this to us. We will then forward an official Agreement for you to sign.

We look forward to hearing from you as soon as possible.

Yours sincerely

Andrew Roach
Sales Manager

Appointing an overseas agent (2)

This letter is well presented, easy to read, and informative.

Softy Fabrics

3 Denmark Rise · Newtown · NE3 1YH
Tel: 3468 714856 · Fax: 3468 718921

```
Your Ref
Our Ref BF/SS/export

25 August 199X

Mr Larry Hooper
American Toys Inc
2390 10th Avenue
New York
NY 1234

Dear Mr Hooper

Further to your order of 12 August 19- - we have
today despatched to you some soft fur material to
the value of 5,000 US Dollars. We present our
Bill of Exchange, drawn on you for this sum at
3 months from today's date, for acceptance and
return.

We hope your business goes well.

Yours sincerely



Sara Smythe (Ms)
```

Handling Bills of Exchange (1)

1. This letter is perfectly correct in all it says. It just doesn't read in a very friendly way. An effort could be made to 'pad it out' a little.

2. The quantity of material and its name or type, should be stated.

3. The enclosure notation ('enc') has been omitted.

Softy Fabrics

3 Denmark Rise · Newtown · NE3 1YH
Tel: 3468 714856 · Fax: 3468 718921

Your Ref
Our Ref BF/SP/export

25 August 199X

Mr Larry Hooper
American Toys Inc
2390 10th Avenue
New York
NY 1234

Dear Mr Hooper

Thank you for your order of 12 August 19--. We
have today despatched to you 20 rolls of Beaver
soft fur material to the value of 5,000 US
Dollars.

We enclose our Bill of Exchange, drawn on you for
this sum at 3 months from today's date, for your
acceptance and return to us.

May we take this opportunity of wishing you every
success in your new venture.

Yours sincerely

Simon Palmer
Management Trainee

enc

Handling Bills of Exchange (2)

This example not only states the facts, but also suggests that Softy are pleased to
be doing business with American Toys. This should encourage favourable
relationships for the future.

POINTS FOR DISCUSSION

1. Why is it important to write in simple language when sending a letter abroad? Do you think it is advisable to write in the language of that country if you are able to?

2. Find out as much as you can about the different ways of transferring money abroad. Make a list of all the ways you can think of and then state at least one advantage and one disadvantage of each.

3. Work with a partner. Both of you write down what you see as being the advantages and disadvantages of selling goods to overseas markets. When you have finished, compare notes and discuss your findings.

11
Letters on Tricky Subjects

INTRODUCTION

Examples of tricky letters could easily fill an entire book, and in fact one such book has been written (see Further Reading). The first point to consider is what constitutes a tricky letter anyway? A letter one person finds difficult to write someone else might find easy, and vice versa.

The aim of this chapter is to show just a few examples of letters that could prove tricky to write. If these are combined with the examples in Chapter 9 (letters to staff can be difficult to compose), you will have a good cross-section to refer to.

It can be tempting, particularly in letters of complaint for instance, to resort to rude and abusive language. Occasionally a sarcastic or cryptic comment can be slipped in, but downright rudeness is not acceptable in any business letter, however fed up you might feel about the situation.

The sample letters
The sample letters in this chapter illustrate the following:

Letter	Pages
Sending a strong letter of complaint	140-141
Dealing with a complaint made to the company	142-143
Terminating a business arrangement	144-145
Asking the bank for a loan	146-147
Writing a letter of sympathy	148-149
Sending a letter of apology	150-151

The Animal Kingdom

Bruin Street, Newtown, NE10 0PY
Telephone: 3691 279017

1 November 199X

Mr Andrew Roach
Sales Manager
Super Toys Ltd
Chattisfield Road
NEWTOWN
NE12 0LD

Dear Mr Roach

I am writing to tell you just how furious I am about the way Jim Brooks has treated my Shop Assistant, Molly, on his last two visits here.

I would have thought you could have trained your sales reps to behave in a civil manner. He was offhand, rude, and abusive. I can only think that this is the way you tell them to behave, because the last one, Mick Jones, didn't behave any better either.

If you are not able to train your reps to behave in a better manner than this, perhaps you are in the wrong job.

Unless you can come up with a good answer for all this we will not trade with you in the future.

Yours sincerely

Jenny Bateman (Miss
Partner

Sending a strong letter of complaint (1)

1. This letter is rude and abusive in its tone, which is just what Jenny is complaining about from one of Andrew's sales reps! Although she is quite obviously furious, her approach needs to be polite and firm, but not rude.

2. A letter such as this is not likely to receive the desired result. It is likely to annoy and upset Andrew. After all, he may not be wholly responsible for his rep's behaviour.

The Animal Kingdom

Bruin Street, Newtown, NE10 0PY
Telephone: 3691 279017

1 November 199X

Mr Andrew Roach
Sales Manager
Super Toys Ltd
Chattisfield Road
NEWTOWN
NE12 0LD

Dear Mr Roach

I am writing to complain about the way Jim Brooks has treated my Shop Assistant, Molly, on his last two visits here.

On both occasions Mr Brooks was offhand, rude, and abusive. His manner caused Molly to feel very upset, which I find disturbing, particularly as the rep who used to call on us before Mr Brooks – Mick Jones – had an equally offputting attitude.

As Sales Manager, I would have thought your main aim was to train your reps to behave in an acceptable manner to their customers. It must, therefore, concern you to know that they are upsetting customers rather than encouraging new business.

I await your comments with interest. I should say that unless you are able to send someone to us who behaves in a friendly, businesslike way, we shall be forced to buy our goods from another company.

Yours sincerely

Jenny Bateman
Partner

Sending a strong letter of complaint (2)

A strong complaint has been made here without resorting to rudeness. This letter should shock Andrew sufficiently to make him take positive action to rectify the situation.

Super Toys Ltd

Chattisfield Road, NEWTON NE12 0LD
Tel: No 2567 591048 Fax: No 2567 651987

4 November 199X

Miss Jenny Bateman
Partner
The Animal Kingdom
Bruin Street
NEWTOWN
NE10 0PY

Dear Miss Bateman

I am extremely sorry that you have found it necessary to write and complain about the behaviour of one of our sales representatives.

Please be assured that I have spoken to Mr Brooks and have given him a very strong warning that if this kind of behaviour ever occurs in the future his position with this company will be in serious jeopardy. In his defence, he says that your assistant, Molly, tried to flirt with him, which was when he became offhand and possibly slightly abusive, but an experienced representative should be able to handle such situations without resorting to rudeness.

If you ever have any trouble in the future, please do not hesitate to contact me immediately.

Yours sincerely

Andrew Roach
Sales Manager

Dealing with a complaint made to the company (1)

1. Although Andrew has apologised and offered some sort of explanation, Jenny is not likely to feel very reassured by this letter.

2. Andrew has not mentioned the fact that Super Toys would not wish to lose The Animal Kingdom's business. This could lead Jenny to believe that they are not bothered one way or the other.

Super Toys Ltd

Chattisfield Road, NEWTON NE12 0LD
Tel: No 2567 591048 Fax: No 2567 651987

4 November 199X

Miss Jenny Bateman
Partner
The Animal Kingdom
Bruin Street
NEWTOWN
NE10 0PY

Dear Miss Bateman

I am extremely sorry that you have found it necessary to write and complain about the behaviour of one of our sales representatives.

Please be assured that I have spoken to Mr Brooks and have given him a very strong warning that if this kind of behaviour ever occurs in the future his position with this company will be in serious jeopardy. In his defence, he says that your assistant, Molly, tried to flirt with him, which was when he became offhand and possibly slightly abusive, but an experienced representative should be able to handle such situations without resorting to rudeness.

I shall call on you myself in the future, so you and your assistant can rest assured that you will have my personal attention at all times. Your business is extremely valuable to us and I would not like to destroy the good relationships we have built up over the years.

My first call to you will be during the afternoon on Wednesday next, 10 November and I look forward to seeing you then.

Yours sincerely

Andrew Roach
Sales Manager

Dealing with a complaint made to the company (2)

Andrew has diffused a tricky situation. Molly, the assistant, says she was treated badly, whilst Jim Brooks, the rep, says she deserved it. By Andrew taking over their calls, the business relationship can continue without further upset.

Softy Fabrics

3 Denmark Rise · Newtown · NE3 1YH
Tel: 3468 714856 · Fax: 3468 718921

Your Ref
Our Ref BF/SS/6301

14 November 199X

Brook & Son Toymakers
61-71 Steel Street
BRIDGETOWN
BR61 7RE

Dear Sirs

As you know we had trouble with you earlier this
year when you wouldn't pay for your goods. We were
forced to take legal proceedings to recover the
money.

This letter is just to tell you that we wish to
terminate any business arrangements with your
company as you are unreliable.

Yours faithfully

Sara Smythe (Ms)
Management Trainee

Terminating a business arrangement (1)

Although Sara states the case in no uncertain way, perhaps a little more tact and
thought could improve the wording!

Softy Fabrics

3 Denmark Rise · Newtown · NE3 1YH
Tel: 3468 714856 · Fax: 3468 718921

Your Ref
Our Ref BF/SP/6301

14 November 199X

Brook & Son Toymakers
61-71 Steel Street
BRIDGETOWN
BR61 7RE

Dear Sirs

You will remember that during the summer of this
year we wrote to you repeatedly asking you to
settle your account with us. At that time you did
not make payment and we were forced to take legal
proceedings.

Although we have now recovered this money, the
time involved and the attitude of your company,
have forced us to make the reluctant decision not
to supply goods to you in the future.

Yours faithfully

Simon Palmer
Management Trainee

Terminating a business arrangement (2)

This version makes the same points as the first one, but it does so in a rather
'softer' way. This company have proved unreliable, but going on about it will not
help now. Refusing to supply them in the future is all that is necessary.

```
┌─────────────────────────────────────────────────────────────────┐
│                                                                   │
│                       The Animal Kingdom                          │
│                    Bruin Street, Newtown, NE10 0PY                │
│                      Telephone: 3691 279017                       │
│                                                                   │
│  20 November 199X                                                 │
│                                                                   │
│  Mr John Price                                                    │
│  Manager                                                          │
│  Stephens Bank                                                    │
│  High Street                                                      │
│  NEWTOWN                                                          │
│  NE25 8JK                                                         │
│                                                                   │
│  Dear Mr Price                                                    │
│                                                                   │
│  I am writing to ask you if you would consider giving us a bank   │
│  loan to enable us to purchase the enclosed retail premises.      │
│  These premises would be opened up as another branch of The       │
│  Animal Kingdom.                                                  │
│                                                                   │
│  As you know, we have been trading successfully here in Newtown   │
│  for seven years now, and we feel there would be a market for our │
│  goods in Churchgate too.                                         │
│                                                                   │
│  We do have 50% of the purchase price to put in ourselves, and    │
│  would need a loan for the remaining 50%, plus an amount to stock  │
│  the new shop. The premises are empty at the moment. Nigel, my    │
│  partner would live in the upstairs flat mentioned in the details.│
│                                                                   │
│  When you have given this letter some thought in principle,       │
│  perhaps we could come in and see you. Our accounts are enclosed  │
│  for the last financial year.                                     │
│                                                                   │
│  Yours sincerely                                                  │
│                                                                   │
│                                                                   │
│                                                                   │
│  Jenny Bateman (Miss)                                             │
│  Partner                                                          │
│                                                                   │
│  enc                                                              │
│                                                                   │
└─────────────────────────────────────────────────────────────────┘
```

Asking the bank for a loan (1)

1. This is Jenny's first draft of what is a tricky letter to write. She now needs to get the facts into some sort of logical order.

2. A subject heading, giving the address of the new premises would help, too.

The Animal Kingdom
Bruin Street, Newtown, NE10 0PY
Telephone: 3691 279017

20 November 199X

Mr John Price
Manager
Stephens Bank
High Street
NEWTOWN
NE25 8JK

Dear Mr Price

Retail Premises – 56-60 High Street   Churchgate

I am writing to ask you if you would consider giving us a bank loan to enable us to purchase the above property, with a view to opening a second branch of The Animal Kingdom.

As you know, we have been trading successfully here in Newtown for seven years now, and we feel there is a market for our goods in Churchgate too. The property we have found is empty and would provide ample retail space, together with an upstairs flat where Nigel, my partner, would live.

The purchase price of the property is £70,000 freehold. We have £35,000 to put in ourselves and would need to borrow the remaining £35,000, plus an amount of say £10,000 towards stocking the new branch.

When you have given this matter some thought in principle, perhaps we could come in and see you.

We are enclosing details of the property together with our audited accounts for the last three years.

Yours sincerely

Jenny Bateman (Miss)
Partner

enc

Asking the bank for a loan (2)

This version is much better. The facts are clearly stated.

Super Toys Ltd

Chattisfield Road, NEWTON NE12 0LD
Tel: No 2567 591048 Fax: No 2567 651987

3 December 199X

Mrs R James
90 Clear View
NEWTOWN
NE16 7YH

Dear Mrs James

Sorry to hear about Phillip's death. It must have been a shock for you.

Hope you have recovered enough to be enjoying life once more.

Yours sincerely

Angie Young (Ms)
PERSONNEL MANAGER

Writing a letter of sympathy (1)

1. Angie has asked Chris Masters to rough this out on her behalf to see what he manages to say. Predictably, he does not show any tact or understanding.

2. Someone receiving this letter would not think that Angie really cares one way or the other about Phillip's death. It is too flippant and lighthearted and does not sound at all sincere.

Super Toys Ltd

Chattisfield Road, NEWTON NE12 0LD
Tel: No 2567 591048 Fax: No 2567 651987

3 December 199X

Mrs R James
90 Clear View
NEWTOWN
NE16 7YH

Dear Mrs James

I was very sorry to hear of Phillip's death. It must have been a great shock to you, as it was to us all here.

Phillip was a valued friend as well as a loyal employee, and we will all miss him very much.

Our thoughts are with you at this difficult time.

Yours sincerely

Angie Young (Ms)
PERSONNEL MANAGER

Writing a letter of sympathy (2)

1. Angie has written this herself and you will see that it is much more sincere.

2. Saying that Phillip was very highly thought of at work should offer some comfort to Mrs James. No words are adequate at a time such as this, but a sincere attempt to show that someone cares can help a little.

The Animal Kingdom

Bruin Street, Newtown, NE10 0PY
Telephone: 3691 279017

4 January 199X

Mrs R Abbott
43 Long Reach
NEWTOWN
NE1 5TH

Dear Mrs Abbott

TIMOTHY TEDDY BEAR

I was very sorry to receive your letter of 2 January complaining about the bear you bought from us to give to your young daughter at Christmas.

We have never had a complaint before with these bears. They are manufactured to a very high standard and I find it difficult to understand how the stuffing could possibly have escaped.

We aim to please, however, so please find enclosed a replacement bear with our compliments.

Yours sincerely

Nigel Flack
Partner

enc

Sending a letter of apology (1)

1. The second paragraph of this letter almost suggests that Mrs Abbott is lying about the problem with her bear. This is not a very good attitude to adopt when sending a letter of apology, particularly when the goods concerned were given to a young child as a present.

2. Jenny tells Nigel that she does not like the wording in this letter and that she feels it would be a good idea for it to be changed. Jenny's version is shown next.

The Animal Kingdom
Bruin Street, Newtown, NE10 0PY
Telephone: 3691 279017

4 January 199X

Mrs R Abbott
43 Long Reach
NEWTOWN
NE1 5TH

Dear Mrs Abbott

TIMOTHY TEDDY BEAR

I am writing to apologise for the problems you have encountered with the bear you purchased from us to give to your daughter at Christmas.

All the bears we stock are manufactured to a very high standard. I therefore find it very disturbing to hear about the stuffing escaping from your particular bear. I can only say that, although this is the first problem we have ever had on this range, we do take your complaint very seriously and will contact the manufacturer for their comments.

In the meantime, please accept a replacement bear and a small gift, with our compliments, along with our sincere apology for the distress caused to yourself and your daughter.

Yours sincerely

Jenny Bateman (Ms)
Partner

enc

Sending a letter of Apology (2)

1. Mrs Abbott should be satisfied with this letter. Giving a small gift as well as a replacement bear shows good faith and a sincere wish to make amends.

2. Jenny has pointed out that complaints are very rare and poor workmanship will not be tolerated at The Animal Kingdom.

POINTS FOR DISCUSSION

1. Why do you think it is most important not to be rude in a business letter? Are there any instances you can think of when rudeness would be acceptable?

2. Compose a letter to your bank manager, telling him or her that your small electronics business is in trouble and you owe quite a lot of money. Say that you are putting your house on the market and should be able to pay off your debts once it is sold, as well as buy something smaller to live in. Say you want to borrow some money – say £10,000 to tide you over. Try to word the letter in such a way that the manager will want to help you.

3. Should a letter of apology be sent to a customer who has complained about something, if you know they are in the wrong and you are in the right?

12
Personal Business Letters

SETTING OUT PERSONAL BUSINESS LETTERS

A personal business letter is a letter written from a private address to a business address. Like any other business letter it needs to be displayed in a way that is clear and easy to read.

Presentation
A typewritten letter looks more impressive than a handwritten one and is a definite must if your writing is difficult to read. You should check first though, just to make sure you are not specifically asked to use your own handwriting for the letter. Centring your home address at the top of the page adds a professional touch; so does the addition of a subject heading where relevant.

Checking
Always read through your letter when you have finished it. Check carefully to make sure that the sentences and paragraphs are well constructed and that there are no careless typing errors to spoil the effect.

Examples
On the following pages you will find a selection of personal business letters for you to read through and adapt to your own needs. At the end of each letter, relevant comments are made for you to bear in mind when constructing your own letters.

The sample letters
The sample letters in this chapter illustrate the following:

River View
Painters Road
Tardley
NORTHDEAN
NO1 9TY

11 March 199X

Mr C Smith
Personnel Manager
Robirth West
Queensway
NORTHDEAN
NO3 6PY

Dear Mr Smith

<u>Senior Assistant to Personnel Manager</u>

I should like to apply for the above position, advertised in the Daily Echo today.

A copy of my Curriculum Vitae is enclosed. From this you will see that I am at present working as a junior assistant in the personnel department at Charles Evans Associates. Although I enjoy my work I feel I would now like to take on a position with more responsibility, and in a larger organisation.

I can be available for interview at any time and I look forward to hearing from you.

Yours sincerely

Julie Youngs (Miss)

Enc

Applying for a job

1. Always state the vacancy applied for. There could be several jobs advertised at the same time.

2. Check whether the letter should be handwritten. If not, a typewritten copy looks best and is easier to read.

3. Do not repeat information given in a CV or application form, although a *short* summary of a particularly relevant point can be made. Always keep the letter as brief as possible.

```
                          River View
                          Painters Road
                          Tardley
                          NORTHDEAN
                          NO1 9TY

2 April 199X

Mr C Smith
Personnel Manager
Robirth West
Queensway
NORTHDEAN
NO3 6PY

Dear Mr Smith

Senior Assistant to Personnel Manager

I am pleased to confirm that I shall be available for interview on Monday
12 April 199X at 1000 hours.

I look forward to meeting you.

Yours sincerely



Julie Youngs (Miss)
```

Attending an interview

1. Keep this type of letter very brief.

2. Make sure the job title, and the day and time of interview are clearly
   mentioned.

The Old Ship
Redweave Road
NORTHDEAN
NO24 1BN

15 April 199X

Mr C Smith
Personnel Manager
Robirth West
Queensway
NORTHDEAN
NO3 6PY

Dear Mr Smith

Julie Youngs

I have known Julie for ten years now. She is a friendly, thoroughly reliable, honest girl, and I am sure she will be a credit to your Company.

Yours sincerely

Martin J Bourne

Writing a letter giving a character reference

1. References, especially character references, can be a little biased, to say the least. It is unlikely that someone who has known you for ten years will say anything outright to ruin your chances of getting the job. Similarly, you will not want to upset a friend by giving them a bad reference, either.

2. If you are not really happy about someone's ability, there are ways of diluting your reference, for instance: 'I have known Julie for ten years now. She is a friendly girl and to the best of my knowledge she is reliable and honest. I have no reason to believe she would be unsuitable for the position.'

River View
Painters Road
Tardley
NORTHDEAN
NO1 9TY

28 April 199X

Mr D Evans
Charles Evans Associates
The Midstreet
NORTHDEAN
NO12 8PY

Dear Mr Evans

This is to give formal notice of my intention to leave Charles Evans Associates. I should like to leave on Friday 28 May, which is one month from today.

Although I shall be sorry to leave the Company, I have, as you know, been offered a senior position at Robirth West. In view of the challenge this position gives me, I have decided to accept their kind offer.

I would like to take this opportunity to thank you for being so helpful and supportive during the last three years.

Yours sincerely

Julie Youngs (Miss)

Writing a letter of resignation

1. Very often a letter of resignation is written with some degree of regret. If so, there is no harm in letting your employer know that you have not taken your decision lightly, and that you do appreciate any help you have been given in the past.

2. Most companies will ask for a period of notice to be worked. This can be anything from one week to three months, although one month's notice is the most usual.

```
                    The Old Ship
                    Redweave Road
                    NORTHDEAN
                    NO24 1BN

20 April 199X

Miss Julie Youngs
River View
Painters Road
Tardley
NORTHDEAN
NO1 9TY

Dear Julie

Congratulations on getting the job at Robirth West. You really deserve it
and I'm sure they will soon realise how lucky they are!

Hope all goes well on the first day. Sue and I look forward to meeting you
for lunch as soon as you have settled in.

Best wishes

Yours sincerely
```

Writing a letter of congratulation

1. With a more personal letter like this one, there is no need to type the name
    under the signature.

2. The inside address (Julie's address) has still been placed at the beginning of
    the letter which suggests that they are not close friends. When sending a
    letter to a close friend this inside address is omitted.

2 The Reaches
Wood View
NORTHDEAN
NO3 1YN

10 June 199X

Mr and Mrs A Abbott
4 Ribble Road
Pottling
NORTHDEAN
NO8 1RT

Dear Mr and Mrs Abbott

I should like to invite you both to the Club's Charity Ball, which is to be held on 10 July 199X at 2000 hrs in the Clubhouse.

I can arrange for up to six complimentary tickets, so that you may bring guests if you wish.

Please would you let me know as soon as possible whether or not you are able to attend, as tickets are strictly limited.

Yours sincerely

David Pringle

Writing a letter of invitation

Invitations, particularly for formal occasions, are often sent by means of printed cards. Letters are just as effective, however, and can be far cheaper to produce.

4 Ribble Road
Pottling
NORTHDEAN
NO8 1RT

14 June 199X

Mr David Pringle
2 The Reaches
Wood View
NORTHDEAN
NO3 1YN

Dear Mr Pringle

Thank you for the kind invitation extended to my wife and myself for this year's Charity Ball.

I am sorry to say, however, that on this occasion we will be unable to attend, as we are away on holiday during July.

Please extend our sincere apologies to the other club members.

Yours sincerely

Tony Abbott

Writing a letter refusing an invitation

1. Always be polite when refusing an invitation.

2. Make sure you give a reason why you cannot attend, even if the reason is invented!

```
                              Super Scissors
                               2 The Close
                                 Nardley
                               NORTHDEAN
                                NO1 9TH


12 July 199X


HM Inspector of Taxes
Northdean 6 District
Halfway House
NORTHDEAN
NO1 9HY


Dear Sirs


Ref No: 156/593/ACT


Despite writing to you on 24 June 199X, I have still not received my
assessment of tax liability for the current year.

Perhaps you would be kind enough to investigate this matter for me, and
confirm that I will not be liable for any interest charges on overdue tax.


Yours faithfully



John Smith
```

Writing to the Inland Revenue

1. This letter begins with Dear Sirs and so finishes with Yours faithfully, rather
    than Yours sincerely.

2. Always quote your tax reference number in such a letter.

3. Many people are very frightened of writing to the Inland Revenue. There is
    no need for this as they are human beings just doing a job, as you are. Be
    polite but forceful, stating your problem as clearly as you can.

```
                        Super Scissors
                        2 The Close
                        Nardley
                        NORTHDEAN
                        NO1 9TH

20 July 199X

HM Customs and Excise
Lodge House
NORTHDEAN
NO2 TYH

Dear Sirs

Visit by Customs and Excise Inspector on 10 August

Thank you for your letter of 15 July, advising me of the above visit.

Unfortunately our business will be closed for annual holidays from 3-17
August, and I shall myself be out of the country on 10 August.

I sincerely apologise for any inconvenience I am causing, but I would be
very grateful if this visit could be re-scheduled to avoid these dates.

Yours faithfully



James Anderson
```

Writing to the Customs and Excise

1. Never give the impression that you are trying to put off a VAT visit for no
   reason. As long as a valid reason is given, Customs and Excise will usually
   be understanding and re-schedule the visit.

2. Always be polite and apologetic in a letter like this. If you treat official
   bodies with respect, they will usually treat you in the same way.

8 The Ridings
Wallsey
NORTHDEAN
NO27 1YB

8 August 199X

Mr T Jenkins
Jenkins & Co Solicitors
Richmond Road
NORTHDEAN
NO6 1PY

Dear Mr Jenkins

<u>16 Water Lane, Porinworth</u>

With regard to our purchase of the above property, we have not yet received the Contract to sign. You did say that this would be with us on Monday of <u>last</u> week.

As the proposed completion date is now only a month away, we should like to know the up to date position.

We have been unsuccessful in our attempts to reach you by telephone. Would you please contact us by the end of this week, so that we can discuss this matter in more detail.

Yours sincerely

Mark Preston

Writing to your solicitor

1. Solicitors are famous for their lack of speed. Every now and then they need an ultimatum to spur them into some sort of action.

2. Make sure you address the letter to the person dealing with your case.

3. Never be rude even if you are feeling really fed up with the service you are receiving. The tone of this letter is sufficiently strong to give out the message that it is time for action.

```
                                        8 The Ridings
                                           Wallsey
                                         NORTHDEAN
                                          NO27 1YB

20 August 199X

Mr R Sedgewick
Manager
Woods Bank Ltd
High Street
NORTHDEAN
NO2 1YN

Dear Mr Sedgewick

Account No: 05621489 – M & A Preston

We received our latest bank statement this morning, and were very
distressed to see that, once again, an amount of £125.00 was deducted by
direct debit on 12 August 199X, for an insurance policy we do not possess.

You may remember that the same discrepancy occurred last month. When
we contacted you then we were told that the amount would be credited and
the matter would be fully investigated.

As you will see, the deduction this month has caused us to go overdrawn.
This, of course, is through no fault of ours, and we do not expect to pay
any of the usual charges for overdrawn accounts.

We would like you to look into this matter urgently and send us an
amended statement. We would also like to know why this keeps happening
and what you intend to do about it.

Yours sincerely


Mark Preston
```

Writing to your bank/building society

1. Always give the account number on correspondence to a bank or building
   society.

2. Do not be rude, but make your point forcefully. You are entitled to ask for
   an explanation, especially as this is the second time the error has been made.

21 Seaview Road
Halton
GREAT WALTON
Norfolk
NO31 6PY

24 August 199X

Mr T Singh
The Lodge
Station Square
GREAT WALTON
Norfolk
NO30 6YN

Dear Mr Singh

You may remember I wrote to you on 3 March 199X regarding urgent repairs which need to be carried out at the above address. I am enclosing a copy of that letter in case it has been mislaid.

The leaking roof is becoming more serious as each day goes by, and this, together with the damp walls and rotting paintwork, is making living conditions very unsuitable, particularly for my small child who suffers from asthma.

Please would you telephone me on 0493-717892 as soon as possible and give me a definite date for these repairs to be carried out. If they are not completed soon I shall have no alternative but to look for alternative accommodation.

Yours sincerely

Jane Meadows (Mrs)

enc

Writing a letter to do with property

1. This type of letter needs to be firm, stating the case in a clear and definite way.

2. The landlord's conscience should be stirred into action by the mention of the small child suffering from asthma.

3. The threat of finding alternative accommodation, may help, as long as alternative accommodation is available and your landlord does not want to lose you as a tenant.

Super Scissors
2 The Close
Nardley
NORTHDEAN
NO1 9TH

1 September 199X

Mrs A Rolt
3 The Steps
Roughton
NORTHDEAN
NO28 9TY

Dear Mrs Rolt

Despite writing to you three weeks ago, we have still not received the £1,200.00 you owe for the dresses we made for you in June of this year. This surprises us as you have always been a reliable customer in the past.

Please send a cheque for this amount by return of post. If we do not receive payment by 21 September, we shall be forced to put this matter into the hands of our solicitor. We regret this action, but feel we have no alternative.

Yours sincerely

James Anderson

Writing a letter about money owed to you

1. Although this letter needs to be firm, an attempt has been made to soften the blow by mentioning the customer's previous good record.

2. The final paragraph should state that the debt needs to be settled immediately and what will happen if it is not.

Hedgerow Corner
Church Road
NORTHDEAN
NO13 7PN

23 September 199X

Mr James Stander
Educational Publisher
Robert Cook & Son
20-24 The Street
LONDON
WE1 5PN

Dear Mr Stander

I am at present working on a book covering all aspects of buying and renovating properties in France. As you will see from the enclosed Synopsis, my aim is to show the reader that French properties make very affordable main or second homes, often in outstanding settings.

I feel this subject is of particular interest at the moment, due to the recent opening of the Channel Tunnel, making travel to France even easier than before.

I have had two other books published. They are 'BUYING A HOUSE ON A BUDGET' and 'CHOOSING YOUR HOLIDAY HOME'. I also write a regular column in Everyday Homebuyer.

If you would like to see a sample chapter, please let me know.

Yours sincerely

Margaret Riff

enc

Writing to a publisher

1. Sending a publisher an outline of your proposal is a far better idea than writing the book first and then sending the finished manuscript. If the idea does not get off the ground you will not have wasted valuable time.

2. Always write to a named person at a publishing house. If necessary telephone first to check who to write to.

3. Remember to say why you think your book will appeal and mention any previous writing experience.

```
                        16 Low Road
                          Heacham
                       GREAT WALTON
                          Norfolk
                        NO30 1CY


14 October 199X

Mr J Green
Editor
The County Journal
20 Ship Street
GREAT WALTON
NO31 1PH

Dear Mr Green

Evergreen Social Club

Please find enclosed a report on our recent meeting.

We would be most grateful if you would publish this report in the County
Journal as soon as space allows.

Many thanks for your help.

Yours sincerely



Maud Scott (Mrs)


enc
```

Writing a letter to a newspaper

1. Most local newspapers are quite happy to publish reports on local
   organisations. They like to appear 'in touch' with the local people.
2. Do not ask for a specific date for publication unless strictly necessary.
3. Remember to thank the Editor in anticipation of his or her help.
4. In the actual report remember to mention the time, date and place of the
   next meeting. You may as well get in some free advertising. After all,
   potential new members may read the report and decide to come along if they
   know when and where to come.

16 Low Road
Heacham
GREAT WALTON
Norfolk
NO30 1CY

12 November 199X

The Rt Hon David Paternoster-Smith MP
House of Commons
LONDON
SW1A 0AA

Dear Mr Paternoster-Smith

THE EVERGREEN CLUB – HEACHAM BRANCH

I am writing to ask if you would consider giving a talk at our Christmas meeting, to be held in the Heacham Village Hall on Wednesday 15 December at 3.00 pm. Our members would be particularly interested to hear you talk about your work as a Cabinet Minister.

As you have visited us before, I do not need to remind you that we are all a little old and frail, but still have lively minds and most of us enjoy politics, especially the afternoon sessions on the television!

We do have substantial club funds and we will gladly pay your expenses if you will agree to give the talk.

We look forward to hearing from you. Please try not to disappoint us!

Yours sincerely

Maud Scott (Mrs)

Writing to your MP

1. This letter is obviously from someone quite elderly who doesn't mind who she approaches in the interests of her club!

2. It is a lively letter and could just appeal to the better nature of the gentleman in question.

3. Generally speaking, a letter to an MP can either be sent to the person's local address or to the House of Commons.

POINTS FOR DISCUSSION

1. 'A typewritten letter gets better results than a handwritten one.' Do you think this statement is true? Give your reasons.

2. Prepare a letter to send to an imaginary travel company complaining about a disastrous holiday. The holiday was in an apartment in Spain. There were lengthy flight delays each way and the apartment was a shambles. The travel company are: Sunnytravel Ltd. Address: 6 The Drive, LITTLETOWN LI1 5CY. Contact Name: Ms Wendy Luck.

3. Prepare a letter to send to an estate agent asking for details of properties. You are looking in the Great Yarmouth area and in the price range £50,000–£70,000. You need three bedrooms and do not wish to live on an estate. Ask to be put on their mailing list, too. The estate agents are: Newroots & Co, 5 The Walk, Great Walton, NO32 9BV.

Appendix
Suggested Answers to Assignments
In Chapters 2–4

CHAPTER 2 PAGE 27

Dear Sir

I wrote to you on 24 July asking if you would let me have 100 copies of your new magazine. I have heard nothing from you and I am beginning to get rather worried.

I hope you will not let me down as I have a number of people waiting for copies, and my reputation is at stake if I do not deliver on time.

If they are not here by Wednesday I shall be forced to cancel the order. This will be a pity as I have dealt with you for many years now.

Yours faithfully

CHAPTER 2 PAGE 28

1   Mr A Jones BA
    41 The Highway
    NORTHDEAN
    NO4 6AZ

2   The date was 29 May 199X and the actual time was 9.30 pm. Mr B Salter decided to take his car to the ABC Garage. He thought his car needed some new parts, eg, brake linings and filters.

CHAPTER 3 PAGE 37

Dear Mr Jones

I am pleased to tell you that the blood samples taken when you came to see me last week proved negative, and you have nothing at all to worry about.

Do let me know if you have any further problems in the future.

Yours sincerely

CHAPTER 4 PAGE 53

Question 1

21 Orbit Road
London
W8 9RT

2 January 19- -

Ms Jane A Prior
Director
Seaside Travel Ltd
65-70 Sunny Street
LITTLETOWN
LI2 7DY

Dear Ms Prior

HOLIDAY IN PORTUGAL – MARCH 199X

With reference to your letter regarding the above holiday, I apologise for not sending the final payment to you but I have been in hospital until very recently.

Although I am now at home, my doctor says I will not be fit to travel in March, and I am enclosing a letter from him explaining the situation.

In view of these exceptional circumstances, do you think it would be possible for you to refund my deposit money which I paid last year?

I look forward to hearing from you.

Yours sincerely

B Smith (Mrs)

enc

Question 2

9 January 199X

Mrs B Smith
21 Orbit Road
LONDON
W8 9RT

Dear Mrs Smith

HOLIDAY IN PORTUGAL – MARCH 199X

Thank you for writing to me about your proposed holiday with us.

I was very sorry to hear of your recent illness and quite understand your reasons for cancelling your booking. I am afraid, however, that we are not in a position to refund your deposit money ourselves. The best plan would be for you to write to our insurance company, Bestway Travel at the address shown on our booking details. They will be able to advise on whether or not you are entitled to a refund. I am returning your doctor's letter for you to send on to them.

I sincerely hope that very soon you will be fully recovered from your illness, and that you will decide to take a holiday with us at a future date.

Yours sincerely

Jane A Prior (Ms)
DIRECTOR

enc

Glossary

Blind copy. A copy of a letter taken for a person other than the recipient and without that recipient's knowledge.

Capital outlay. Money required to buy business assets.

Cash on delivery (COD). A business term which means that goods will be paid for at the time they are delivered to the customer.

Circular letter. An identical letter sent out to many different people, often over a period of time rather than all on the same day.

Communication. The process by which we give, receive or exchange information with others.

Complimentary close. The ending of a letter. Usually 'Yours faithfully' or 'Yours sincerely'.

Continuation sheet. A second or subsequent sheet of a letter.

Customer. Person or organisation buying goods or services.

Data. Information

Database. Recorded data which can be retrieved and updated.

Disk. Storage medium used by many computers. Can be 'floppy' or 'hard'.

Draft. The first, rough copy of a document.

Embolden. To show a word/words in bold type.

Enquiry. A customer asks a supplier for details of goods or services available. This usually takes the form of a letter of enquiry.

Franking. By means of a franking machine a 'franking' showing the postage paid and possibly an advertising slogan too, can be automatically printed onto an envelope, eliminating the need for traditional stamps.

Fully blocked layout. Type of layout in which every line of text begins at the left margin.

Grammar. Rules and usages of language that help us to speak or write correctly.

Hard copy. Printout (on paper).

Indented. Text sets in from the left and/or right margin.

Invoice. A business document giving details of goods or services supplied to a customer, and their price.

Junk mail. Mass produced leaflets, circulars, letters etc, usually advertising products or services.

Justified text. Text which has completely straight left and right margins.

Keying in. A term used to indicate the use of a keyboard for producing a typewritten copy of a document.

Layout. The way a document is displayed.

Letterhead. Printed headed paper of a company or other organisation.

Limited company. A popular form of business organisation, owned by its shareholders and managed by its directors. It can be either a private limited company (Ltd after the name), or a public limited company (plc after the name). In a private limited company the owners put money in by buying shares. In a public limited company the shares are sold to the general public, often through the Stock Exchange.

Logo. Printed design or pattern used as an emblem on a company letterhead.

Mailmerge. A 'mailmerge' means combining two or more computer files to produce several different documents; eg a database containing names and addresses could be merged with a standard letter producing many individual letters.

Media. A term generally used to mean television, radio and the press.

Memorandum (memo). A memo is a written communication like a letter. Unlike a letter, however a memo is usually an internal document, passing from one department of a company to another.

Open punctuation. The use of no punctuation at all unless absolutely necessary. In business letters this means the only punctuation comes in the main body of the letter (not in the address, salutation or signatory details).

Order. A written request to supply goods or services.

Paragraph. One or more sentences grouped around a central theme or subject.

Pitch sizes. The size of type used to produce a document. The commonest ones are 10 pitch and 12 pitch.

Program. The instructions written to make a computer obey certain commands.

Proofread. To check text carefully for mistakes.

Quotation. A written description of goods or services to be supplied with prices and usually stating estimated delivery times.

Recipient. A person who receives something.

Running costs. Operating expenses for example of machinery.

Salutation. The beginning of a letter. Usually Dear Sir/Madam or Dear Mr/Mrs/Ms . . . .

Sentence. A set of words containing a subject and a predicate. The subject is the person or thing being discussed. The predicate says something about the subject.

Signatory. The person signing a letter.

Standard letter. A letter sent out to many different people containing the same basic information.

Statement. A business document sent by a supplier to a customer, giving details of all transactions that have taken place over a specified period and any outstanding amounts of money.

Supplier. Person or organisation providing goods or services to a customer.

Terms of settlement. A business term indicating the time allowed for payment of goods or services, eg '30 days net'.

Transmit. To send or pass on.

Waffle. 'Flowery' language using unnecessary words and not getting straight to the point.

Window envelope. An envelope containing a 'window' or transparent covering to allow the address of the recipient to show through from

Further Reading

Business Letters Made to Measure, Derek and Joan Perkins (Domino Books).

Collins Office Handbook (Harper Collins).

Debrett's Correct Form, edited by Patrick Montague-Smith (Headline Books).

How to Manage Computers at Work, Graham Jones (How To Books).

How to Master Business English, Michael Bennie (How To Books, 2nd edition).

How to Write a Report, John Bowden (How To Books, 2nd edition).

Letter Writing, Nigel Rees, (Bloomsbury).

Mind the Stop, G.V. Carey (Penguin). A complete guide to punctuation.

Pitman Business Correspondence, G. Whitehead and D. H. Whitehead (Pitman Publishing).

Secretarial Duties, John Harrison (Pitman).

Readymade Business Letters, Jim Dening (Kogan Page).

Titles and Forms of Address: A Complete Guide to Their Correct Use (A. & C. Black).

Tricky Business Letters, Gordon Wainwright (Pitman Publishing).

Index

How to Master Business English
Michael Bennie

Are you communicating effectively? Do your business documents achieve the results you want? Or are they too often ignored or misunderstood? Good communication is the key to success in any business. Whether you are trying to sell a product, answer a query or complaint, or persuade colleagues, the way you express yourself is often as important as what you say. With lots of examples, checklists and questionnaires to help you, this book will speed you on your way, whether as manager, executive, or business student. Michael Bennie is an English graduate with many years' practical experience of business communication both in government and industry. He is Director of Studies of the Department of Business Writing of Writers College, and author of *How to Do Your Own Advertising* in this series.

208pp illus. 1 85703 129 6. 2nd edition.

How to Master Public Speaking
Anne Nicholls

Speaking well in public is one of the most useful skills any of us can acquire. People who can often become leaders in their business, profession or community, and the envy of their friends and colleagues. Whether you are a nervous novice or a practised pro, this step-by-step handbook tells you everything you need to know to master this highly prized communication skill. Contents: Preface, being a skilled communicator, preparation, researching your audience, preparing a speech, finding a voice, body language and non-verbal communication, dealing with nerves, audiovisual aids, the physical environment, putting it all together on the day, audience feedback, dealing with the media, glossary, further reading, useful contacts, index. 'An excellent read – I recommend it wholeheartedly.' *Phoenix/ Association of Graduate Careers Advisory Services.*

160pp illus. 1 85703 149 0. 3rd edition.

How to Pass That Interview
Judith Johnstone

Everyone knows how to shine at interview — or do they? When every candidate becomes the perfect clone of the one before, you have to have that extra 'something' to raise your chances above the rest. Using a systematic and practical approach, this How To book takes you step-by-step through the essential pre-interview groundwork, the interview encounter itself, and what you can learn from the experience afterwards. The book contains sample pre- and post-interview correspondence, and is complete with a guide to further reading, glossary of terms, and index. A Graduate of the Institute of Personnel & Development, Judith Johnstone has been an instructor in Business Studies and adult literacy tutor, and has long experience of helping people at work.

128pp illus. 1 85703 118 0. 2nd edition.

How to Keep Business Accounts
Peter Taylor

A third fully revised edition of an easy-to-understand handbook for all business owners and managers. 'Will help you sort out the best way to carry out double entry book-keeping, as well as providing a clear step-by-step guide to accounting procedures.' *Mind Your Own Business*. 'Progresses through the steps to be taken to maintain an effective double entry book-keeping system with the minimum of bother.' *The Accounting Technician*. 'Compulsory reading.' *Manager, National Westminster Bank (Midlands)*. Peter Taylor is a Fellow of the Institute of Chartered Accountants, and of the Chartered Association of Certified Accountants. He has many years' practical experience of advising small businesses.

176pp illus. 85703 111 3. 3rd edition.

How to Master Book-Keeping
Peter Marshall

Book-keeping can seem a confusing subject for people coming to it for the first time. Now in a newly revised edition, this very clear book will be welcomed by everyone wanting a really user-friendly guide to recording business transactions step-by-step. Illustrated at every stage with specimen entries, the book will also be an ideal companion for students taking LCCI, RSA, BTEC, accountancy technician and similar courses at schools, colleges or training centres. Typical business transactions are used to illustrate all the essential theory, practice and skills required to be effective in a real business setting. Peter Marshall has been Tutor in Education at the University of Lancaster and Director of Studies at the Careers College, Cardiff.

176pp illus. 1 85703 065 6. 2nd edition.

How to Manage Computers at work
Graham Jones

Most books on computers are highly technical, and often tied in to one particular application or product. This book really is different. Assuming no prior knowledge, it is a practical step-by-step guide which puts the business needs of the user first. It discusses why a computer may be needed, how to choose the right one and instal it properly; how to process letters and documents, manage accounts, and handle customer and other records and mailing lists. It also explains how to use computers for business presentations, and desktop publishing. If you are not sure how to start, then this is definitely the book for you . . . and you don't need an electronics degree to start! 'Bags of information in a lingo we can all understand. I strongly recommend the book.' *Progress/NEBS Management Association*. Graham Jones has long experience of handling personal computers for small business management and is Managing Director of a desktop publishing company.

160pp illus. 1 85703 078 8.

How to Do Your Own Advertising
Michael Bennie

This book is for anyone who needs — or wants — to advertise effectively, but does not want to pay agency rates. Michal Bennie is Director of Studies at the Copywriting School. 'An absolute must for everyone running their own small business... Essential reading... Here at last is a practical accessible handbook which will make sure your product or service gets the publicity it deserves.' *Great Ideas Newsletter (Business Innovations Research)*. 'Explains how to put together a simple yet successful advertisment or brochure with the minimum of outside help... amply filled with examples and case studies.' *First Voice (National Federation of Self Employed and Small Business)*.

176pp illus. 0 7463 0579 6.

How to Write a Press Release
Peter Bartram

Every day, newspapers and magazines are deluged with thousands of press releases. Which stories make an editor sit up and take notice? Why do some press releases never get used? The author knows from more than 20 years' first-hand experience in journalism what turns a release from scrap paper into hot news. This book takes you through every stage of the process from conceiving the story idea, researching the information and writing the release, to distributing it by the most effective means. If you have ever had a press release rejected – or want to win 'free' column inches for your organisation – *How to Write a Press Release* is the handbook for you. Peter Bartram BSc(Econ) is one of Britain's most published business writers and journalists, with more than 2,500 feature articles and seven books to his credit. He edits the magazine *Executive Strategy*.

160pp illus. 1 85703 069 9.

How to Write a Report
John Bowden

Communicating effectively on paper is an essential skill for today's business or professional person for example in managing an organisation, staffing, sales and marketing, production, computer operations, financial planning and reporting, feasibility studies and business innovation. Written by an experienced manager and staff trainer, this well-presented hand book provides a very clear step-by-step framework for every individual, whether dealing with professional colleagues, customers, clients, suppliers or junior or senior staff. Contents: Preparation and planning. Collecting and handling information. Writing the report: principles and techniques. Improving your thinking. Improving presentation. Achieving a good writing style. Making effective use of English. How to choose and use illustrations. Choosing paper, covers and binding. Appendices (examples, techniques, check-lists), glossary, index.

160pp illus. 1 85703 124 5. 2nd edition.